ALSO BY PHILLIP STEPHEN SCHULZ

America the Beautiful Cookbook

As American as Apple Pie

Cooking with Fire & Smoke

Cooking for Giving (with Bert Greene)

Vodka 'n' Vittles

CELEBRATING AMERICA

A *Cookbook*

PHILLIP STEPHEN SCHULZ

SIMON & SCHUSTER

NEW YORK LONDON TORONTO

SYDNEY TOKYO SINGAPORE

SIMON & SCHUSTER

ROCKEFELLER CENTER

1230 AVENUE OF THE AMERICAS

NEW YORK, NEW YORK 10020

DESIGNED BY PEI LOI KOAY

MANUFACTURED IN THE UNITED STATES OF AMERICA

3   5   7   9   10   8   6   4   2

LIBRARY OF CONGRESS CATALOGING-IN-PUBLICATION DATA

SCHULZ, PHILLIP STEPHEN.

CELEBRATING AMERICA : A COOKBOOK / BY PHILLIP STEPHEN SCHULZ.

P.   CM.

INCLUDES BIBLIOGRAPHICAL REFERENCES AND INDEX.

1. COOKERY, AMERICAN.   2. HOLIDAY COOKERY—UNITED

STATES.   3. FESTIVALS—UNITED STATES.   I. TITLE.

TX715.S2989   1994

641.5973—DC20   93-8662

CIP

ISBN 0-671-70189-4

FOR GEORGE C. MOSKOWITZ

ACKNOWLEDGMENTS

✳

AS ALWAYS, I am grateful to Judith Blahnik for being there when I needed her. Thanks to Kerri Conan and Toula Polygalaktos, who tried to show me the way when the subject matter seemed overwhelming—and to Sydny Miner, who saw the book through its final stages. Thanks also to the various state agricultural department heads and assorted festival directors for all their help. The number of festivals in this country, food and otherwise, is simply staggering. Serious festival followers—and they are legion—might also find the following books of interest: *Festivals U.S.A.*, by Kathleen Thompson Hill (John Wiley & Sons, Inc.); the Landau Communications series of festivals *(California Festivals, Festivals of New England, Festivals of the Pacific Northwest, Festivals of the Southwest)* published in San Francisco; and, especially for food lovers, *Food Festival,* by Alice M. Geffen and Carole Berglie (Pantheon).

CONTENTS

❋

INTRODUCTION

✳

MAN HAS BEEN celebrating special days and events since the beginning of recorded history and, undoubtedly, long before that. The four seasons were surely early demarcations of time passing, and as mankind progressed and agricultural societies developed, the harvest took its proper place in the yearly cycle of life. As nations evolved, historical milestones most often became the reason for celebrations. In our own country, for instance, Forefathers' Day, December 21, commemorates the day that the Pilgrims landed in the New World at Plymouth Rock. And Independence Day, our most patriotic holiday, is celebrated with picnics and barbecues on July 4—the day the Continental Congress officially approved the Declaration of Independence. America's unique role as a "melting pot" has also had its impact. Since the majority of Americans have roots in other countries, holidays like St. Patrick's Day, which honors the patron saint of Ireland, and the Day of Our Lady of Guadalupe, which honors the patron saint of Mexico, are also celebrated here.

On an individual level, we tend to place our own special meanings on the holidays. Each of us has a special Christmas, Thanksgiving, or Fourth of July that we remember fondly. It's funny how we most often remember ourselves as kids, back home with Mom and Dad, nary a care in the world, just livin' on Mom's home cookin'. We cling to the dates of special events, as well. I'll never forget the year ('86–'87 season) the Mets and (football) Giants gave New Yorkers a whole lot to remember; nor July 14, 1966—Bastille Day, as well as my nephew John's ninth birthday. It was also the day I was drafted into the U.S. Army. I had to leave John's birthday party early in order to board the train for El Paso, Texas, and Fort Bliss (a misnomer if ever there was one).

Officially, there are ten *legal* federal holidays in America. All federal government offices are closed on these occasions, with many state and local governments following suit. They are New Year's Day, Martin Luther King, Jr.'s Birthday, George Washington's Birthday, Memorial Day, Independence Day, Labor Day, Columbus Day, Veterans Day, Thanksgiving Day, and Christmas Day. Half of these holidays are celebrated on the Monday nearest the actual date of the event—an idea dreamed up by the federal government to give workers (and department stores) some additional three-day weekends. It was also tried once with Veterans Day, but there was such an uproar that the holiday was returned to November 11.

Christmas Day is the only religious feast day that is also a designated federal holiday. While some religious festivals are identified with saints (St. David's Day and St. Nicholas's Day, for example), others (such as Passover and Easter) are observed in honor of significant religious events. Still other celebrations have religious roots but have lost much of their religious relevance over the years: Halloween, Mardi Gras, and Valentine's Day, for example.

A day of celebrating no doubt seemed most appropriate to the Pilgrims who survived to observe their first harvest celebration. That first celebration took place in September or October. Our modern-day Thanksgiving holiday wasn't officially relegated to the fourth Thursday in November until 1941.

Fall, being harvest time, contains more festivals than the other seasons. The last of the summer vegetables have been gathered; crisp rosy apples and golden pumpkins are at the ready. Wintertime harvest festivals are hard to come by, but you can head west and get in on a carrot festival, or if you prefer, go to the desert and savor fresh dates. Fortunately, there are quite a few feast days and holidays in winter to make up for the lack of harvest festivals. Spring, of course, starts another cycle. The maple sap is running; so are the shad and salmon. Then, as the strawberries are ripening on the vine, we start enjoying the summer harvests of cherries, blueberries, onions, garlic, beans—and even watermelon in a town called Hope, Arkansas.

If the holidays and festivals selected for this book seem a bit eclectic, they just might be. I have tried to choose the obvious, as well as the fun and interesting, ones. After all, in some people's minds, frogs and alligators make just as fine dining as lamb, beef, or oysters. A calf fry, on the other hand, is listed solely for the adventurous. The recipes that are included reflect traditional dishes associated with these holidays and festivals. For instance, Plymouth Succotash, a stew of poultry, meat, beans, and corn, was served at the very first Forefathers' Day celebration in 1796. A modern-day rendition may be found under Forefathers' Day in the "Fall" section of this book. And what could be more appropriate than the recipe for Cherry Triangles included under the "National Cherry Festival" heading in the "Summer" section of the book?

So join the celebration. And if your travels take you to any of the harvest festivals listed in this book, be sure to say hello—and taste a little something for me.

SPRING RECIPES

❈

SPRING

❋

S P R I N G .   A time for birth and renewal. A time to rake, turn, and fertilize the soil, and then to plant. It is the season of grass growing and trees leafing. Our heads are filled with visions of asparagus vinaigrette, roasted lamb, sautéed fiddlehead ferns, Easter ham, rhubarb pie, shad and salmon runs, and all else that heralds the spring season.

I remember two things about the springs of my Colorado childhood: my father's garden, with its budding corn, peas, beans, squash, carrots, and lettuce; and the restorative veneer of green on the otherwise austere (and brown) landscape of the foothills just west of Denver. It was a greening that did not last long, I might add. Life in the dry zone does have its drawbacks. For the last twenty-one years, however, I have spent most of my springs on Long Island's South Fork—springs that, unlike Colorado's, are incredibly lush and green. And amidst that greenery, the trees (cherry, apple, pear, dogwood) don a blanket of blossoms as if to celebrate yet another winter's passing. It is a lushness made possible by the high humidity that comes with the territory, and it's well worth the occasional discomfort, in my opinion.

I do not claim to have a green thumb, though most of my problems stem from the fact that my garden plots are inevitably overshadowed by gigantic trees. My herbs do fine and my impatiens thrive, but my vegetables inevitably turn out to be sadly scrawny. My father's garden, on the other hand, was legendary. I don't remember the exact size of the garden plot, but it was large enough that a nearby farmer had to be called on to turn the soil over with his tractor. It was a serious garden that required serious work, and we kids had to do our share, hoeing and planting. My father, who died in 1991, carefully laid out the rows using wooden stakes and string for a guide. We helped put the seeds in the holes he made. Every garden has its weeds, of course, and I really didn't mind pulling them, but, for the most part, the weeding chores came my way only after the plants had grown a bit. For you see, I once pulled up all the tiny corn plants by mistake, thinking they were weeds. I think I am alive today simply because my father was just too astonished to kill me.

Looking back, those spring days now seem hopelessly bucolic. Perhaps they were. We lived in the shadow of Castle Rock in Golden, Colorado. Ours was the last house on a road that dead-ended at two giant cottonwood trees smack at the foot of Table Mountain. That mountain was our playground. Sitting between Denver and its environs, it served as a wedge against suburban sprawl, keeping the town rural. An irrigation ditch lay between our house and the hillside. It not only provided water, but was a beacon for the cattle and horses kept at bay by a somewhat rickety barbed-wire fence. Often, as we sat on the porch while dusk turned to darkness, the cattle stood lowing, staring longingly with their big liquid eyes. Sadly, only houses stand there now.

❋

■ MARCH ■

With rushing winds and gloomy skies
The dark and stubborn Winter dies;
Far-off, unseen, Spring faintly cries,
Bidding her earliest child arise;
March!

—BAYARD TAYLOR

In early Roman times, March was the first month, coinciding with the beginning of the agricultural cycle. In 153 B.C., January 1 was designated as the day officials took office and hence became the beginning of the civil year. It did not become legally binding, however, until the Julian calendar was introduced in 46 B.C.

✳

■ MARCH SPECIAL EVENTS ■

NATIONAL PEANUT MONTH: Sponsored by the peanut-growing states of the South. The NPM Committee asserts that during this one month alone, Americans down 60 million pounds of snack-type peanuts, 50 million pounds of peanut-based candy, and 1 *billion* peanut butter–and–jelly sandwiches. That's just nuts!

NATIONAL FROZEN FOOD MONTH: Sponsored by the National Frozen Food Association to let the public know how economical and convenient frozen foods are.

NATIONAL NUTRITION MONTH: Sponsored by the American Dietetic Association to remind the public that frozen foods really are economical and convenient. Information on cholesterol and fat reduction, weight reduction, and understanding product labels, as well as shopping tips, are available by phone. The number is (800) 366-1655.

✳

ST. DAVID'S DAY —
MARCH 1

ST. DAVID is the patron saint of Wales, and the Welsh in America have been celebrating his day ever since they arrived here. A large number of Welsh migrated to this country in the 1800s, pouring into industrial areas like Wilkes-Barre, Scranton, and Pittsburgh, Pennsylvania. But Welsh settlers were here long before that. As a matter of fact, more than fifty signers of the Declaration of Independence were of Welsh descent, including its author, Thomas Jefferson. While some say that St. David came from a well-to-do family and later turned to the church, others have claimed that his mother was a nun who had been raped by the Devil. He studied the Bible assiduously in his youth and became deeply religious. Eventually, he either founded or restored twelve monasteries in England. On a lighter note, however, he will always be associated with leeks. Yes, leeks. As one story has it, while doing battle against the Saxons, St. David had his men wear leeks in their hats so they could be readily recognized—a custom that survives on St. David's Day, both in Liverpool and in Philadelphia.

▪ POTATO AND LEEK SOUP ▪

This soup is similar to a chowder. If you wish, you may puree the mixture, thinning it with milk as needed, and serve it well chilled.

3 large leeks, washed and finely
   chopped
2 tablespoons vegetable oil
1 large clove garlic, minced
½ teaspoon chopped fresh thyme, or
   pinch dried thyme
1 small carrot, finely grated
1 small bay leaf

3 medium potatoes (about 1½ pounds),
   peeled and cubed
2 cups milk
2 cups chicken broth
Salt and freshly ground pepper
Dash hot pepper sauce
Chopped fresh parsley

1. In a large heavy pot, sauté the leeks in the oil over medium-low heat for 2 minutes. Add the garlic; cook for 2 minutes. Stir in the thyme, carrot, and bay leaf. Cook, covered, for 5 minutes.

2. Add the potatoes to the pot and stir in the milk and chicken broth. Heat to boiling, stirring often. Reduce the heat and cook, covered, until the potatoes are tender, 12 to 15 minutes.

3. Remove the bay leaf from the soup. Transfer about 1 cup of soup (mostly potatoes) to a food processor or blender. Process until smooth; be careful, as hot liquid will expand. Stir the puree back into the soup and add salt, pepper, and hot pepper sauce to taste. Serve hot, garnished with parsley.

SERVES 4

GUILD INDIAN FAIR — FIRST WEEKEND IN MARCH

EVERY YEAR, more than 40,000 folks descend on the Heard Museum in Phoenix, Arizona, to celebrate the art and lives of the American Indian. The big draws here are the original works of art and the crafts of the Native Americans who partake in this fair. In fact, this is one of the most important shows of Indian arts and crafts in the United States. The jewelry, pottery, weavings, beadwork, sculptures, and paintings for sale are of very high quality and attract buyers from all over the country. When not shopping for treasures, you can take in the Indian tribal dances and sample some mighty fine Native American cuisine. There are fry breads, either soaked in honey or piled high with spicy beef and tomatoes, *posole,* blue popcorn, Hopi *piki* bread, and hot tamales, to name just a few of the available dishes. For more information, contact the Heard Museum at (602) 252-8848.

■ POSOLE ■

Posole *is a stew made of hominy, meat, and chile peppers. The following uses ancho chiles (dried poblanos), which are widely available these days.*

2 pounds beef chuck steak or brisket,
   or pork shoulder
4 cups chicken broth or water
3 ancho chiles (dried poblanos)
2 tablespoons vegetable or olive oil

1 medium onion, chopped
1 clove garlic, minced
2 cans (16 ounces each) white hominy,
   drained and rinsed

1. Place the meat in a heavy pot just large enough to hold it. Add the chicken broth. Heat to boiling, reduce the heat, and cook, covered, over medium-low heat until the meat is barely tender, about 2 hours. Remove the meat from the broth and let it cool slightly on a plate; reserve the broth. Trim any fat from the meat and cut it into ½-inch pieces.

2. Meanwhile, remove the stems from the chiles and slit them open with a sharp knife. Discard the seeds. Place the peppers in a small saucepan and add just enough water to cover. Heat to boiling, reduce the heat, and simmer until tender, about 15 minutes. Transfer the peppers and liquid to a food processor or blender and process until smooth. Add some meat broth if more liquid is needed.

3. Heat the oil in a heavy medium-size pot over medium-low heat. Add the onion; cook for 1 minute. Add the garlic; cook for 4 minutes. Stir in the chile puree, the meat, hominy, and 2 cups of meat broth. Stir well and heat to boiling. Reduce the heat and simmer, partially covered, until the *posole* is thick and the meat and hominy are very tender, about 1 hour. Add more broth as needed.

SERVES 4

❋

✳

LUTHER BURBANK'S BIRTHDAY—
MARCH 7

BORN IN 1849 in Lancaster, Massachusetts, Luther Burbank grew up to be one of America's most important agronomists. He began with market gardening on a small scale and developed a new variety of the potato (the Burbank) while still quite young. By the ripe old age of twenty-six, Burbank had set up a nursery in Santa Rosa, California, where he experimented with flowers, fruits, and vegetables. He gave the nursery up while he was in his early forties and devoted himself full-time to experimentation and the development of new plants.

Even though Burbank wasn't even born when the potato blight struck Germany in the 1840s, this disastrous phenomenon would profoundly affect his life. Most of us know what happened when the blight jumped to Ireland, where this important food crop was devastated year after year. It has been estimated that more than a million people died in the two decades following the first blight. The blight was also prevalent in America, and in 1859, to make matters worse, potato beetles appeared in Colorado and quickly spread eastward. Burbank, working with the Early Rose potato plant, developed a strain that was blight resistant. (His foes would later claim that the plant he "developed" was from an already developed pod seed of the Early Rose potato.) In any case, the Burbank potato went on to become one of the most planted potatoes of all times. It is commonly referred to as the Idaho potato and is also known as the russet and the russet Burbank.

■ HEAVENLY POTATO GNOCCHI ■

Making gnocchi is the best use of leftover mashed potatoes ever thought of by man. And mashed potatoes are best made with mealy baking potatoes like Idahos. The secret to making gnocchi is to keep the board and your hands well floured at all times. I freeze these on baking sheets and then slip them into self-seal bags for safekeeping until ready to use. Just reheat in a 400° F oven for about 20 minutes before serving.

3 cups cold mashed cooked potatoes
½ cup (1 stick) unsalted butter, melted
2 egg yolks, lightly beaten
½ cup grated Swiss or Parmesan cheese

1 cup all-purpose flour plus extra
⅛ teaspoon freshly grated nutmeg
Salt and freshly ground white pepper

1. Place the potatoes in a large bowl and stir in ¼ cup butter, the egg yolks, and the cheese. Stir in 1 cup flour, the nutmeg, and salt and pepper to taste. Add extra flour, if needed, to form a soft dough. Roll into ropes on a well-floured board and slice into 1-inch lengths. Press the ends of the gnocchi with the tines of a fork.

2. Drop the dumplings, 8 to 10 at a time, into a large pot of boiling, salted water. Return water to simmering and cook the gnocchi until they float to the surface and are firm, about 1 minute. Remove with a slotted spoon and drain on paper towels. Place on a lightly buttered heatproof serving dish. Continue until all dough is used up.

3. Preheat oven to 350° F (400° F if frozen). Drizzle the remaining ¼ cup melted butter over the gnocchi and bake until slightly puffed, about 15 minutes (20, if frozen).

SERVES 6

✳

ST. PATRICK'S DAY— MARCH 17

IT SEEMS that on St. Patrick's Day, the whole world is Irish—wearin' the green, eatin' corned beef and cabbage, drinkin' Irish coffee, and what not. In olden days, St. Patrick's Day parades in cities like Boston, New York, and Chicago were boisterous, rough-and-tumble affairs. They're a bit more subdued today but are still popular and generally attract large crowds.

St. Patrick, of course, is the patron saint of Ireland, even though he was, ironically, British. He was born in the Severn Valley in Britain around A.D. 389. The Irish kidnapped him when he was sixteen and sold him into slavery. When he escaped six years later, he vowed to return to Ireland—which he did in 432, as a bishop. He then proceeded to convert much of the country to Christianity. One of the reasons the shamrock is associated with the day is that St. Patrick used its three leaves to explain the Holy Trinity.

For some time now, there has been a rumor that Irish coffee was actually invented at the bar of the St. Francis Hotel in San Francisco. Not so, according to Eugene McSweeney of the Lacken House in Kilkenny, Ireland. Mr. McSweeney claims that it was created by a bartender named Joe Sheridan, who worked at the pub at the Shannon Airport. It seems that one cold morning, waiting passengers asked for hot toddies to break the chill. Using what he happened to have on hand—coffee, brown sugar, whiskey, and some cream—Sheridan invented Irish coffee on the spot.

▪ IRISH COFFEE ▪

*D*on't forget the following toast, which McSweeney says should be served with the coffee:

St. Patrick was a gentleman
Who through strategy and stealth,
Drove all the snakes from Ireland
Here's a toasting to his health.
But not too many toastings lest
You lose yourself and then,
Forget the good St. Patrick and
See all those snakes again!

Hot strong black coffee
1 teaspoon brown sugar
1 jigger Irish whiskey (plus 1 drop in
  honor of Joe Sheridan)

¼ cup (approximately) heavy cream,
  lightly whipped

Warm an 8-ounce glass with hot tap water. Discard the water and fill the glass about seven-eighths full with coffee. Add the sugar and whiskey and stir until the sugar has dissolved. Gently pour the cream over the back of a spoon onto the surface of the coffee so that it floats on top and forms a "collar" on the glass.

SERVES 1

❋

VERNAL EQUINOX—ON OR ABOUT MARCH 22

The vernal equinox occurs about March 22, when the sun crosses the plane of the equator and night and day are of equal length all over the earth. From this point until fall (the autumnal equinox) in the Northern Hemisphere, the days will be longer than the nights. The longest day, and the end of spring, coincides with the arrival of the summer solstice (about June 22).

❈

❈

PECAN DAY— MARCH 25

ON THIS DAY in 1775, George Washington planted pecan trees at Mount Vernon. Some of those trees (a gift from Thomas Jefferson) flourish to this day. The pecan is native to the American South. It is interesting to note that about 22 percent of the pecans grown in this country come from wild, or native, trees. The remaining 78 percent have been cultivated for easy picking and have thin shells. Georgia is the largest pecan-producing state, followed by New Mexico, Alabama, Texas, Louisiana, and Florida.

▪ WILD RICE AND PECAN PILAF ▪

The following is an original recipe from Marilyn Harris, a dear friend, whose syndicated radio show, "Cooking with Marilyn," originates daily from WCKY in Cincinnati. In addition to being one of the hottest on-air personalities in the Midwest, Marilyn writes a weekly food column for the Cincinnati Enquirer *and is the author of two cookbooks, her latest being* More Cooking with Marilyn *(Paxton Press).*

2 tablespoons unsalted butter
1 large shallot, minced
⅓ cup wild rice
1¼ cups water
½ cup long-grain white rice
¾ cup homemade beef stock or canned
　beef broth
¼ cup white wine

1 small bay leaf
Dash hot pepper sauce
½ cup frozen peas, thawed
2 tablespoons chopped fresh parsley
¼ cup pecan halves, toasted and
　coarsely chopped (see Note)
1 teaspoon chopped fresh mint
　(optional)

1. Melt the butter in a medium-size saucepan over medium heat. Add the shallot; cook for 2 minutes. Stir in the wild rice and the water, and heat to boiling. Reduce the heat to medium-low and simmer, covered, for 30 minutes.

2. Add the white rice, beef stock, wine, bay leaf, and hot pepper sauce to the wild rice. Heat to boiling, then reduce the heat to medium-low. Simmer, covered, until the rice is tender and almost all the liquid has been absorbed, about 25 minutes. Discard the bay leaf. Stir the peas into the mixture; cook, covered, for 5 minutes. Remove the cover and raise the heat slightly if the mixture is too wet. Toss in the parsley and pecans, and sprinkle with the mint, if you like.

SERVES 4

N O T E : To toast the pecans, heat a small skillet over medium heat. Add the nuts and toast until golden, stirring frequently, 6 to 8 minutes.

✳

FOR FORTY YEARS, Tucson, Arizona, celebrated its Mexican heritage with La Fiesta del Presidio, one of the best food festivals around. The whole town was turned into a wonderful outdoor *mercado* (marketplace). It still is, but now the fiesta's committee has recently joined forces with the sponsors of Pioneer Days, a festival that honored the pioneer (cowboy) spirit of the region. The result: the Tucson Festival, which celebrates the Indian, Spanish, and pioneer roots of the city. There is a wide variety of entertainment: bands play rock and roll, polka, country western, jazz, and Mexican folk music. There are myriad arts and crafts exhibits, dance troupes, and *vaqueros* (costumed horseback riders). The food is representative of every region of Mexico. You can even sample *menudo,* a soup made of tripe (touted as a hangover cure), and wash it down with *orchata,* a drink made with milk and honey. For more information, contact the Tucson Festival at (602) 622-6911.

▪ SALSA DE POBLANO ▪

*A*s far as I am concerned, a Mexican dish is only as good as its salsa. This recipe calls for *poblano peppers, one of the tastiest—yet not terribly hot—Southwestern peppers. Incidentally, this salsa goes wonderfully well with fried catfish (see page 45).*

2 poblano peppers	Juice of 1 large lime
1 large firm, ripe tomato	3 tablespoons olive oil
1 tablespoon finely chopped onion	Salt and freshly ground pepper
1 large clove garlic, minced	2 tablespoons chopped fresh cilantro

1. Roast the peppers over a gas flame or under a broiler until blackened all over. Carefully wrap the peppers in paper towels and place them in a plastic bag. Let them cool for 5 minutes. Rub off the blackened skin with more paper towels. Discard the seeds.

2. Chop the peppers and place them in a medium bowl. Add the remaining ingredients. Let stand at least 1 hour before serving.

MAKES ABOUT 1 ¾ CUPS

■ APRIL ■

Again the blackbirds sing; the streams
Wake, laughing, from their winter dreams,
And tremble in the April showers
The tassels of the maple flowers.

—JOHN GREENLEAF WHITTIER
"THE SINGER," 1871

The name of the fourth month is believed to stem from the word *aperire,*

Latin for "to open"—just as buds do. Easter and Passover generally fall in

April, coinciding with spring festivals around the world.

※

PASSOVER —
MARCH/APRIL

PASSOVER BEGINS on the fourteenth day of Nisan, the seventh month of the lunar calendar, and lasts eight days. Passover commemorates the night, as related in the book of Exodus, when the angel of death "passed over" the houses of the Egyptians and Israelites, killing the first-born children of the Egyptians, but sparing the Israelite children, whose houses had been marked with the blood of a lamb. This happened on the night that the Israelites escaped from Egypt.

The celebration traditionally begins with the Seder meal, served on the first two days of Passover. *Seder* means "order of service," and the reading of the *Haggadah*—the narration of the Exodus—is an integral part of this meal. Every member of the family—and friends, as well—takes part in the ceremony as the story of the Exodus is told through recitations, chants, songs, and prayers. A plate is set out near the head of the household for the ceremonial Seder foods. Three matzoth, each covered with a napkin and stacked one on another, represent the Bread of Affliction and the unity of the three branches of the Hebrew faith: the Kohanites, Levites, and Israelites. A roasted lamb bone symbolizes the sacrifice of the Paschal Lamb. A roasted egg is a symbol of the ancient festival offering. The *moror* (bitter herbs) recalls the bitterness of slavery. Sweet herbs (parsley) represent spring and growth. Bowls of salt water symbolize tears shed by enslaved peoples. And a mixture of apples, nuts, and wine called *charoseth* symbolizes the mortar that Jewish forefathers used to build "the treasured cities of Pharaoh."

Matzoth, made of wheat flour and water and baked according to strict guidelines for Passover, are symbolic of the unleavened bread the Israelites ate in the desert after their escape from Egypt. No leavening of any kind can be used during Passover. When ground, the waferlike bread is called *matzo meal,* which is used to replace all other flour and grain. (Potato starch can be used, since it is a vegetable and not a grain.)

I felt a trifle awkward at my first seder—a bit guilty, perhaps. My father was a Lutheran minister, and I was brought up in a strict, religious household. However, since Christians also trace their roots back to the Old Testament, I was on familiar ground. In fact, early Christians celebrated Passover as well as Easter. This Seder was not a heavy-handed ceremony but a joyous celebration. Better yet, it was a family affair—not blood family (although there were those there, too) but a collection of friends from all walks of life and all corners of the religious spectrum. I had a great time—and was delighted to be asked again. The second time, I even brought the matzo balls for the soup.

▪ CHICKEN SOUP WITH MATZO BALLS ▪

I learned to make matzo balls at the elbow of my late mentor and dearest friend, Bert Greene. What amazed me most, if I recall correctly, was the rendering of the schmaltz (chicken fat). It truly is one of those kitchen wonders—water turning to fat, right before your eyes.

1 chicken (about 3½ to 4 pounds)	Salt
Matzo Balls (recipe follows)	10 peppercorns
1 clove garlic	3½ cups chicken broth
1 whole onion with skin	
2 whole cloves	GARNISH (OPTIONAL)
1 large carrot, cut into quarters	1 chopped onion
1 stalk celery with leaves, broken	1 chopped medium turnip
1 medium white turnip, quartered	1 chopped parsnip
1 large parsnip, quartered	1 chopped carrot
2 sprigs parsley	Freshly ground pepper
2 tablespoons chopped fresh dill	Chopped fresh dill
1 slice lemon	

1. With a sharp scissors, remove all fat and excess skin from the cavity and neck area of the chicken. Cut off the tips of each wing. Peel the neck and scrape off any

fat. (You should have about ⅔ cup fat altogether.) Wrap the chicken and refrigerate it until ready to use.

2. Place the chicken fat, skin fat, and wing tips in a small saucepan. Add ½ cup water. Heat to simmering; simmer slowly over low heat for about 30 minutes. As the water is absorbed, it will be replaced by chicken fat in the pan. When it begins to sizzle, the fat is rendered. Remove the fat by spoonfuls until you have 3 table-spoons. Chill for 30 minutes.

3. Make the Matzo Balls.

4. Place the chicken in a large, heavy pot. Add the garlic, whole onion, cloves, carrot, celery, turnip, parsnip, parsley, dill, the lemon slice, 2 teaspoons salt, the peppercorns, chicken broth, and water to cover. Heat to boiling, reduce the heat, and simmer over medium-low heat until tender, about 1 hour. Remove scum and fat with a spoon as they rise to the surface. When the chicken is tender, remove it from the pot. Increase the heat and boil the liquid for 10 minutes. (Reserve the chicken for use at another time; see Note.)

5. Strain the soup and return it to the heat. Add the optional vegetables, reduce the heat, and simmer until tender, about 15 minutes. Add salt and freshly ground pepper to taste. Add the Matzo Balls and cook for 10 minutes. Garnish with chopped dill; ladle the soup into bowls and add one matzo ball to each bowl.

SERVES 8 TO 10

NOTE: To reheat the chicken, place it, covered, in a 275° oven for about 15 minutes. Then, place it skin side up under the broiler until the skin crackles, about 5 minutes.

MATZO BALLS

3 eggs
6 tablespoons cold club soda
3 tablespoons rendered chicken fat (see preceding recipe)

Salt
Pinch ground white pepper
$2/3$ cup matzo meal (approximately)
3 quarts water

1. Lightly beat the eggs in a medium bowl. Beat in the club soda, chicken fat, and salt and white pepper to taste. Slowly beat in ¼ cup matzo meal. Add more matzo meal, 2 tablespoons at a time, until the mixture has the consistency of soft mashed potatoes. Cover and chill for 5 hours.

2. Heat the water to boiling. With wet hands, shape the matzo mixture into balls about 1½ inches in diameter. Drop them into the boiling water; reduce the heat to medium and simmer for 25 minutes. Remove the balls with a slotted spoon; let them cool. Refrigerate until ready to use. Remove from refrigerator 30 minutes before heating in soup.

MAKES 10

✳

EASTER — MARCH / APRIL

EASTER SUNDAY is the most important holy day in the Christian calendar. It commemorates the resurrection of Christ following his death on the cross on Good Friday and is celebrated with fairs and processions all over the world. The flowers and brightly painted eggs associated with Easter are said to be fertility symbols, left over from ancient pagan rites honoring the renewal of spring. Even the holiday's name is thought to stem from Eostre or Ostara, the Anglo-Saxon goddess of spring.

Easter (as determined by the Council of Nicaea in A.D. 325) is observed on the Sunday after the first full moon on or following the vernal equinox—from March 22 to April 25. This date also determines Lent, Shrove Tuesday, Ash Wednesday, and so forth.

On Easter morning, when I was a young boy, we kids would wake up to find presents, usually books or coloring books, under our beds. Later in the day we hunted for the Easter eggs that were hidden around the house. We always attended church on Easter, and after church, my mother would serve Easter dinner for the entire family. We were a big family—eight kids—so it wasn't long before one table wasn't large enough and card tables were added for the younger crowd. My mother inevitably served ham, candied sweet potatoes, mashed potatoes, and string beans, but what I remember most about those meals, embarrassed though I should be to admit it, are the eggs made out of Jell-O. They were truly amazing. To make them, Mom poked a hole in one end of an egg and barely pricked the other end with a needle. She would then blow the egg right out of the shell by blowing on the pricked end. After she rinsed and dried the empty egg shells, she filled them with Jell-O, taped the ends, and put them in the refrigerator until they set. She peeled them just before dinner and served them for dessert. (Nowadays, you can buy plastic molds.)

▪ MY FAVORITE HAM ▪

I received the bulk of my culinary education working with the late Bert Greene at "The Store in Amagansett" from 1972 to 1976. "The Store" was, according to the Wall Street Journal, *the very first "gourmet" takeout food store in the U.S. All I know is that it was already famous when I found my way into its busy kitchen and very popular with the tony Hamptons set on Long Island's South Fork. In case you aren't lucky enough to have an original copy of* The Store Cookbook *on hand, the following recipe is for the ham we sold there. I still make it frequently. It is excellent for Easter.*

One 10- to 12-pound boneless ham
   (Dubuque Fleur De Lis is excellent)
Whole cloves
¼ cup Dijon mustard

1 clove garlic, crushed
¼ cup Chinese duck sauce
Dash orange juice
½ cup light brown sugar

1. Preheat the oven to 400° F.

2. Score the top (fatty side) of the ham in a diamond pattern. Place a whole clove at each intersection. Place the ham on a rack in a foil-lined roasting pan.

3. Combine the mustard, garlic, duck sauce, and enough orange juice to make the sauce slightly syrupy. Spread over the top and sides of the ham. Sprinkle the top and sides with brown sugar. Bake for 1½ hours, or until dark brown and ham is heated all the way through. Let stand at room temperature for at least 15 minutes before serving.

SERVES 12 OR MORE

✳

APRIL FOOLS' DAY — APRIL 1

NO ONE is quite sure where the notion for this holiday came from, but it became popular in France after the Gregorian calendar was adopted in 1564 and New Year's Day was shifted from the end of March (which was then March 25) to January 1. Until that time, April 1 was a day for gift giving. As the story goes, those who fought the change (and lost the battle) were mocked every April 1 thereafter with phony gifts—or gifts fit for fools, if you will. These days, people are still playing tricks and telling tall tales or out-and-out lies in an attempt to catch one off guard. But beware: According to some beliefs, if some dope tells you your shoelaces are untied (and they're not) or your zipper is open (and it's not), and it happens to be past noon, *they* are the fools and not you (even if you *did* look).

In France, "fools" are dubbed *poisson d'avril,* or "April fish," though why is a matter of conjecture. It might be because the sun is leaving the zodiacal sign of Pisces at that time. Then again, as is oft said, "April fish are easily caught"—and just as easily cooked for dinner.

■ BROILED OR GRILLED FISH FILLETS ■ WITH ROUILLE

¼ cup olive oil
1 shallot, minced
2 teaspoons chopped fresh chervil or
  tarragon

8 fish fillets (about 8 ounces each)
Processor Rouille (recipe follows)

1. Heat the oil in a small saucepan over medium-low heat. Add the shallot and cook, stirring occasionally, until soft, about 10 minutes. Do not brown. Remove from the heat and cool for 5 minutes.

2. Add the chervil to the shallot mixture. Brush the fish lightly with the mixture and broil or grill over very high heat until crisp, 1 to 2 minutes per side. Serve with Processor Rouille.

SERVES 6 TO 8

PROCESSOR ROUILLE

1 medium potato (about 5 ounces),
  peeled and chopped
½ cup chicken broth
1 small red bell pepper, seeded and
  roughly chopped
3 cloves garlic
3 jarred hot cherry peppers, well
  drained, stems removed

1 jar (2 ounces) pimientos, well drained
1 teaspoon chopped fresh basil
¼ teaspoon chopped fresh thyme or
  pinch dried thyme
¼ teaspoon red-wine vinegar
Dash hot pepper sauce
5 tablespoons olive oil (approximately)
Salt and freshly ground pepper

1. Place the potato and chicken broth in a medium saucepan. Heat to boiling, reduce the heat, and simmer until the potato is barely tender. Add the red pepper. Cook 3 minutes longer. Drain, reserving the broth. Return the broth to the saucepan and keep hot over low heat.

2. Fit a food processor with a steel blade. With the motor running, drop the garlic through the feed tube. Add the cherry peppers, pimientos, potato and red pepper mixture, basil, thyme, vinegar, and hot pepper sauce. Process until smooth.

3. With the motor running, slowly add the oil, 1 tablespoon at a time, until the mixture thickens. Remove the *rouille* from the processor and whisk in 2 to 3 tablespoons of reserved chicken broth. Add salt and pepper to taste.

MAKES ABOUT 1 ½ CUPS

✳

THOMAS JEFFERSON'S BIRTHDAY—APRIL 13

BORN IN 1743, Thomas Jefferson, the third president of the United States, was perhaps the nation's first true gastronome. He introduced vanilla and macaroni to the country, along with Parmesan cheese and French-style (custard-based) ice cream. His love of good food and great wine was renowned.

After the Revolution, he was appointed ambassador to France, which reinforced his "gourmet" image. When he returned home, he was accused by his political rival Patrick Henry of having "abjured his native victuals." But the truth was, he never lost his taste for such homespun goodies as candied sweet potatoes, black-eyed peas, turnip greens, and Virginia ham. Even in Paris, Jefferson mixed and matched American and French cuisines, to the delight of anyone fortunate enough to be invited to his table. He was an avid gardener and laid out his grounds at Monticello with a collection of vegetables, fruits, herbs, and nut trees that were unequaled in the entire thirteen colonies.

During Jefferson's presidency, the hospitality of the White House was so generous that the budget for entertaining actually exceeded Jefferson's annual salary of $25,000. He picked up the tab—and continued to entertain lavishly at Monticello even after his retirement from public life. Though Monticello was sold after Jefferson's death and went through a period of decline, it has since been restored, along with Jefferson's gardens, and is open to the public every day except Christmas. For more information, contact Monticello at (804) 295-8181.

▪ PIGEON SOUP ▪

*I*n Jefferson's day, wild pigeons were plentiful in the woods around Monticello and were used *in numerous ways. The following recipe for pigeon soup is unusual in that the pigeon is braised first, resulting in a stronger flavor. Passenger pigeons, believe it or not, were once so plentiful all one had to do was walk in the woods and club them over the head. Rock Cornish hens or game birds such as quail make fine substitutes.*

2 tablespoons vegetable oil or unsalted
   butter
2 small pigeons or game birds (about 1
   pound each), split down the back
2 large parsnips, chopped
2 large carrots, chopped
2 leeks, washed well and chopped
2 medium ribs celery, chopped

½ teaspoon chopped fresh thyme, or
   pinch dried thyme
6 cups chicken stock
2 cups heavy cream
½ cup soft fresh bread crumbs
½ cup shredded fresh spinach
Pinch cayenne
Salt and freshly ground pepper

1. Heat the oil in a large heavy saucepan over medium heat. Sauté the birds, skin side down, until lightly browned. Sprinkle with the parsnip, carrot, leek, celery, and thyme. Reduce the heat to low. Cook, covered, for 50 minutes.

2. Add the chicken stock to the pot and heat to boiling. Reduce the heat and simmer, covered, for 30 minutes. Remove from the heat.

3. Transfer the birds to a plate and let them cool. Strain the stock into another pan, pressing on the vegetables to release all the juices. When the birds are cool enough to handle, remove the meat from the bones.

4. Stir the cream and the bread crumbs together until smooth. Stir into the stock. Heat to boiling, reduce the heat to low, and simmer, uncovered, 5 minutes. Add the spinach and cayenne; cook 5 minutes longer. Stir the meat into the soup and cook until warmed through, about 5 minutes. Add salt and pepper to taste.

SERVES 6

✳

VERMONT MAPLE FESTIVAL—
THIRD WEEKEND IN APRIL

AS NOTED ELSEWHERE in this book, I am one of Vermont's biggest fans, but it is not with blind allegiance that I state that Vermont produces the world's best maple syrup. My taste buds tell me so. Perhaps it is the weather there—the sap rises best when there is still snow on the ground and the freezing nights give way to warm sunny days. There are actually quite a few sugar-maple festivals throughout the Northeast, but one that attracts more than 35,000 people annually takes place in St. Albans, Vermont. You can learn how maple syrup is made, watch a sap-boiling demonstration, and sample a variety of maple products, including maple sugar, maple fudge, maple cream, maple cotton candy, sugar on snow, and fried bread dipped in maple syrup. Other delights might include maple cupcakes, maple cheesecakes, maple bread puddings, and ice cream sundaes smothered in maple syrup. There is a cooking contest and a pancake breakfast, in addition to arts-and-crafts exhibits and much more. For more information, contact the Vermont Maple Festival Council, Inc., at (802) 524-5800.

▪ MAPLE BREAD PUDDING ▪

It's no secret that I like bread pudding—truly, one of the most inventive uses of leftovers I know of. The following is easy and quite delicious.

One 8-ounce loaf crusty French bread, torn into pieces

2 cups milk

1 cup heavy cream

4 large eggs

1 cup sugar

4 tablespoons (½ stick) unsalted butter, melted

⅔ cup maple syrup

1 sweet apple, peeled and finely chopped

½ cup seedless raisins

1. Preheat the oven to 350° F. Grease a 9-inch square glass dish about 2 inches deep.

2. Place the bread in a large bowl. Stir in the milk and cream. Let stand for 10 minutes.

3. In a medium bowl, whisk the eggs with the sugar until light. Whisk in the butter and maple syrup. Add to the bread mixture along with the apple and raisins. Mix thoroughly.

4. Spoon the mixture into the prepared dish and bake until set, about 55 minutes. Run under the broiler to brown the top.

SERVES 6 TO 8

★   ★   ★

WORLD CATFISH FESTIVAL—
FIRST SATURDAY IN APRIL

ONE OF THE MORE ENDURING (and endearing) images of the American South is that of a boy in overalls and floppy straw hat (à la Huck Finn) lolling on a riverbank fishing for catfish. As romantic as that notion is, most of the catfish we eat today is farm-raised, developed from channel catfish and fed grains, unlike "mud puppies," which are scavengers that feed along river bottoms. Raising catfish is big business in Belzoni, Mississippi, where millions of pounds of the fish are raised each year in more than 22,000 acres of ponds. The catfish festival is held at (and around) the courthouse in Belzoni, which lies about seventy-five miles north of Jackson. There is live entertainment, a fiddling contest, catfish eating contest, a 10-kilometer race, and a free tour of local catfish ponds for those who are interested. The highlight of the festival, however, is the fried-catfish "dinner." Complete with hush puppies,

cole slaw, and that favorite southern beverage, Coca-Cola, the dinner is actually served for lunch. (Take note that when Easter falls on the first Sunday of April, the festival is moved back one week.) For more information, contact the Belzoni Chamber of Commerce at (601) 247-4838.

▪ SIMPLE FRIED CATFISH ▪

*F*ried catfish is excellent served with nothing but a healthy splash of lemon juice or vinegar —or, for that matter, some good old hot sauce. If you're feeling a bit adventurous, however, try some Salsa de Poblano (page 30). You are in for a treat.

½ cup all-purpose flour
½ teaspoon salt
¼ teaspoon freshly ground pepper
Pinch cayenne
2 eggs, lightly beaten
1 tablespoon water

1¼ cups white cornmeal
  (approximately)
2 pounds catfish fillets
4 to 6 tablespoons vegetable oil
Lemon wedges

1. Combine the flour with the salt, black pepper, and cayenne on a plate. Beat the eggs with the water in a shallow bowl. Place the cornmeal on another plate. Dust the fish lightly with the flour, dip it in the eggs, shaking off any excess, and coat lightly with cornmeal. Place on a plate lined with waxed paper.

2. Heat the oil in a large heavy skillet over medium heat until hot but not smoking. Fry the fish, a few pieces at a time, until golden brown, about 2 minutes on each side. Drain lightly on paper towels and keep warm in the oven until all the fillets are cooked. Serve with lemon wedges.

SERVES 4

❋

✳

ARBOR DAY (EARTH DAY) —
APRIL 22

NEBRASKA WAS the first state to celebrate Arbor Day. The first celebration actually took place on April 10. The year was 1872, and the celebration was the brainchild of J. Sterling Morton, a member of the State Agriculture Board. The purpose was to encourage citizens to plant trees in a relatively treeless state. A million trees were planted in the first year. Within twenty years, one hundred thousand acres of wasteland had been turned into forest. Arbor Day is celebrated on different days around the country. In some states it's observed on Luther Burbank's birthday, March 7, in recognition of his horticultural and agronomical achievements. John Chapman, also known as Johnny Appleseed, is also frequently honored on Arbor Day for establishing apple orchards throughout the East and Midwest.

The first major Earth Day celebration took place on April 22, 1970. The message: "Give earth a chance." The purpose: to promote environmental issues and concerns. Not all ecological groups celebrate Earth Day on the 22nd, however. Some observe the day on the vernal equinox.

▪ WALDORF SALAD ▪

This recipe, supposedly invented at New York's Waldorf-Astoria Hotel, is appropriate for any Arbor Day celebration, since both apple and nut trees play a large part.

3 firm red apples
1 tablespoon lemon juice
2 ribs celery, sliced
½ cup coarsely chopped walnuts or
  pecans

½ cup mayonnaise
2 to 3 tablespoons milk
Lettuce leaves

1. Core the apples and cut them into cubes. Place in a large bowl and sprinkle with lemon juice. Toss well. Add the celery and nuts. Toss once more.

2. Whisk the mayonnaise with enough milk to thin, and pour over the salad. Toss well and serve on lettuce leaves.

SERVES 4

❋

THE AREA AROUND Stockton, California, produces close to 70 percent of the entire U.S. asparagus crop—and when the crop is in, the folks of Stockton put on a show no asparagus lover wants to miss. This annual harvest festival attracts more than 70,000 people, who come to chow down on this premier spring vegetable. Asparagus appears in almost every guise, including grilled asparagus, deep-fried asparagus, asparagus sandwiches, asparagus soup, and asparagus salads. The food booths are lined up in a narrow row that is affectionately dubbed "asparagus alley." For more information, contact the Asparagus Festival at (209) 466-6674.

▪ GRILLED ASPARAGUS ▪

This is one of my all-time spring favorites, and it impresses guests no end. I grill the asparagus before the steaks or chops and keep them warm in a low oven.

1 pound fresh asparagus	⅛ teaspoon chopped fresh thyme
¼ cup olive oil	1 teaspoon chopped fresh parsley
4 large fresh basil leaves, chopped	1 small scallion, minced

   1. Break the tough bottoms off the asparagus spears by bending each spear until it snaps. Peel the stems. Place the asparagus in a shallow glass or ceramic dish.

   2. Combine the remaining ingredients and pour over the asparagus. Toss to coat. Let stand, covered, for 30 minutes.

   3. Grill the asparagus over high heat for 10 minutes, turning once. If the stalks are thick, move them to the cooler edges of the grill and continue to cook until crisp-tender.

SERVES 4

■ MAY ■

Spring's last-born darling clear-eyed, sweet,
Pauses a moment, with twinkling feet,
And golden locks in breezy play,
Half teasing and half tender, to repeat
Her song of "May."

—SUSAN COOLIDGE

May was the third month of the old Roman calendar. The name is believed to have come from Maia, the mother of Mercury, or Hermes. May was traditionally considered an unlucky time for marriage, as the month also celebrated the festival of the unhappy dead and the festival of the goddess of chastity—hence, the popularity of June weddings.

❋

■ MAY SPECIAL EVENTS ■

NATIONAL BARBECUE MONTH: Sponsored by the Barbecue Industry Association to get people out of the kitchen and to the grill earlier in the season.

NATIONAL DUCKLING MONTH: Sponsored by Concord Farms in Concord, North Carolina, to teach consumers how to cook and enjoy duckling. There is also a national cook-off.

NATIONAL EGG MONTH: Sponsored by the American Egg Board to promote the nutritional values of the "incredible, edible egg."

THIS FESTIVAL, twenty years old in 1993, is held every year at the Howard County Fairgrounds in West Friendship, Maryland. Breeders bring in their best to show (nearly thirty different breeds), so it's a great place for sheep lovers. There are seminars on virtually everything you ever wanted to know about sheep (and a few on what you didn't): shearing, fleecing, sewing, spinning, dying, and design seminars, to mention just a few. There is entertainment, including a sheepdog demonstration; contests, including the Maryland Grand Lamb Cook-Off; and auctions, for both sheep and one-of-a-kind shawls. For more information, contact the Howard County Tourism Council at (800) 288-8747.

■ SHISH KEBABS TERIYAKI ■

*B*arbecued lamb and shish kebabs seem to be the perennial favorites at the festival. The *following is an invention of Vicki Campbell, who was junior finalist at the 1987 cook-off.*

¼ cup soy sauce

¼ cup red-wine vinegar

¼ cup vegetable oil

1 clove garlic, minced

¼ teaspoon ground ginger

1 pound boneless lamb, cut into 1-inch cubes

4 cherry tomatoes

1 green bell pepper, cut into 1-inch pieces

1 can (8 ounces) pineapple chunks, drained

1 can (8 ounces) whole water chestnuts, drained

Hot cooked rice

Chopped fresh parsley

1. In a shallow glass or ceramic dish, combine the soy sauce, vinegar, vegetable oil, garlic, and ginger. Add the meat. Mix well and refrigerate, covered, for several hours or overnight. Let stand at room temperature for at least 30 minutes before continuing.

2. Remove the lamb from marinade and arrange it on four skewers, alternating with tomatoes, pepper, pineapple chunks, and chestnuts. Grill, or broil, 3 minutes per side for medium-rare. Serve on hot cooked rice, sprinkled with parsley.

SERVES 4

＊

MAY DAY —
MAY 1

THE BEGINNING of May was an important feast time for the Romans. One feast, Floralia, was devoted to the goddess of flowers, Flora. Trees that were, and are, symbols of nature's spiritual vitality played a role as well. Traditionally, the young men of Rome would venture into the woods to select the perfect tree for the occasion. The tree was then brought into town, trimmed of its lower branches, and wrapped round and round with violets. In England, it became the custom for young women, carrying flower-filled baskets, to dance and prance around this "Maypole." At one time, before Puritanism swept the land, young couples paired off and spent the night in the woods "maying together."

May Day in America has had a revival, but strictly on a local basis. I can personally attest to the wonderment of the annual Maypole that finds its way to Riverside Park on Manhattan's Upper West Side. It is nothing fancy to be sure, propped up by some rather large rocks. Just the sight of it, though, somehow makes the world a nicer place to be.

▪ DIVINITY ▪

On May Day it is now traditional for young girls to make paper baskets and fill them with flowers and small gifts for friends and relatives. These small gifts are quite often homemade candy, and no candy is more appreciated than the Divinity that follows. The recipe is adapted from a wonderful book called Candy Hits *by ZaSu Pitts. It was published in 1963 by Duell, Sloan and Pearce, an affiliate of Meredith Press, and now out of print, but it is worth looking for—it's a classic.*

2 cups sugar	2 egg whites
½ cup light corn syrup	1 teaspoon vanilla extract
½ cup water	1 cup chopped nuts
¼ teaspoon salt	

1. In a heavy 3-quart saucepan, combine the sugar, syrup, water, and salt. Heat, stirring, until the mixture is boiling and the sugar has melted. Boil until the mixture reaches the hard-ball stage—250° F on a candy thermometer. Remove from the heat and set aside. Do not stir.

2. In the large bowl of an electric mixer, beat the egg whites until stiff. On high speed, slowly pour in the syrup. Add the vanilla, and continue beating until the mixture forms soft peaks and begins to hold its shape. Add the nuts and pour into a buttered 8-inch-square pan. Let harden and cut into 1-inch pieces.

MAKES ABOUT 20 PIECES

THE SHAD is a member of the herring family, but averages from 4 to 7 pounds and has quite a distinctive taste. It is highly prized for its roe. Shad, like salmon, are born in fresh water, spend most of their lives in salt water, and then return to their birthplace to spawn. Although the season varies and the fish may very well begin their "run" in April, most of the action along Connecticut rivers takes place in May and June. The town of Windsor, a few miles north of Hartford on the Farmington River, just happens to be on the route and hosts the annual Shad Derby Festival. Though the derby itself takes place during May, the third Saturday of the month has been designated Shad Derby Day. Most of the action—the arts and crafts show, the parade, and the food booths—takes place on (or around) the village green, a short walk from the river. The highlight of the day is the "shad dinner" served on the green between 11 A.M. and 3 P.M. The shad is baked and served with just a slice of lemon, coleslaw, and a roll. Dessert can be purchased from one of the food booths. For more information, contact the Windsor Chamber of Commerce at (201) 688-5165.

■ BROILED SHAD ■

One of the easiest ways to prepare shad is to broil it. Shad has an impossible amount of bones, and you will be spared a lot of grief if you have your fishmonger bone and split the fish for you.

1 whole shad (3 to 4 pounds), boned and split	2 tablespoons unsalted butter
1 tablespoon lemon juice	Salt and freshly ground pepper
1 tablespoon all-purpose flour	1 tablespoon chopped fresh parsley
1 teaspoon vegetable oil	Lemon wedges

1. Preheat the broiler. Rub the cavity of the boned shad with lemon juice. Let stand at least 20 minutes. Dust lightly with flour.

2. Rub a baking sheet or a well-used fish plank lightly with oil. Place the shad, skin-side down, on top. Dot with butter and sprinkle with salt and pepper. Broil about 3 or 4 inches from the flame, basting with more butter if needed, until the meat flakes easily when pierced with a fork, about 8 to 10 minutes. Garnish with chopped parsley and serve with lemon wedges.

SERVES 3 OR 4

ID ALFITR is the feast day that ends Ramadan, the Muslim high holy month in which God is said to have revealed the Koran to Muhammad in the seventh century. During Ramadan, Muslims must abstain from all food and liquids from the first light of sunup until sundown. Each day, believers eat only an early-morning breakfast (4:00 A.M.), most often consisting of yogurt and fruit, and a late-evening meal (after sundown) of hearty soup or stew to gain the strength required for the month-long fasting cycle. Ramadan is not just a period of fasting, however. It is a time for reflection and for restraint, for community spirit and kindness to all—a healing time. The cycle is broken only when the new moon reappears.

The morning after the new moon is sighted, Muslims celebrate the *Id Alfitr,* or the feast of fast breaking. It is a day of thanksgiving, gift giving, visiting, and eating. Sweets symbolize the joy believers received during Ramadan. Middle Eastern Muslims make honey-and-nut–filled goodies like baklava and *knafa.* Indian and Pakistani Muslims make a noodle pudding called *sevyan.*

▪ SEVYAN ▪

This unusual pudding is very simple to make, but it does require sevyan *noodles, which are very delicate vermicelli-like noodles, available at Indian grocers.*

2 tablespoons unsalted butter	1 cup sugar
1 cardamom seed, crushed	3 tablespoons sliced almonds
7 ounces *sevyan* noodles	1/3 cup seedless raisins
2 1/2 cups milk	1 tablespoon chopped shelled pistachios

1. Melt the butter in a large saucepan over medium-low heat. Add the cardamom and noodles. Cook, breaking up the noodles with a spoon, 2 minutes. Add the milk and heat slowly to boiling. Reduce heat to low; cook 3 minutes. Add the remaining ingredients and continue to cook, stirring frequently, 5 minutes longer.

2. Spoon mixture into a large serving dish. Cool on a rack. Refrigerate covered at least 1 hour before serving.

SERVES 4 TO 6

✳

THE KENTUCKY DERBY is the big event of the year for the residents of Louisville. Modeled on England's Epsom Derby, this race for three-year-olds has been run at Louisville since 1875. The week that precedes the Derby is hectic and gay, and everyone who is anyone throws a party. Heck, even if you're not anyone, you throw a party. People tend to serve whatever catches their fancy, and not that long ago, burgoo, a stew originally made with squirrel meat, was the traditional Derby dish. But to this day, the proper way to kick off *any* Derby party is with a frosted glass, or silver cup, of mint julep. No one is quite sure why mint juleps have become associated with the Kentucky Derby, but they have been a bluegrass tradition since before the Civil War.

▪ MINT JULEP ▪

Everyone knows that the proper way to serve a julep is in a silver mug. There is great controversy, however, over the matter of the fresh mint. Should the leaves be crushed to release their pungent aroma, or merely bruised? Some Southerners add a dash of bitters, as well.

10 mint leaves	2½ ounces good bourbon
2 teaspoons superfine sugar	3 mint leaves on stem
4 teaspoons water	

1. Partially tear the ten mint leaves and place them in the bottom of a tall 12-ounce glass or silver julep mug. Add the sugar and water and crush the leaves in the sugar mixture with the back of a spoon until well mixed. Fill the glass with finely cracked ice. Add the bourbon and stir. Add more ice to fill to the brim.

Continued on next page

2. Partially tear the remaining mint leaves on their stems and insert into the ice. It is traditional to serve mint juleps with a short straw so that the imbiber gets the full effect of the heady mint aroma.

SERVES 1

✳

MOTHER'S DAY —
SECOND SUNDAY IN MAY

ANNA M. JARVIS lived from 1864 to 1948 and has often been credited with creating Mother's Day in this country. She was a minister's daughter who taught Sunday School in Grafton, West Virginia, and she was very devoted to her mother. After her mother died, Anna began a letter-writing campaign to ministers, businessmen, and congressmen in an effort to get Mother's Day established. She started with a memorial service for her own mother in 1908. Her mother had a fondness for carnations, so vast numbers of white carnations decorated the church where the service was held, and carnations were quickly accepted as the official flower of Mother's Day. The day became celebrated more and more for "living" mothers, however, and red carnations were substituted for white.

In 1913, the House of Representatives adopted a resolution designating the second Sunday in May as Mother's Day. It passed both houses, and on May 9, 1914, President Woodrow Wilson issued the first Mother's Day proclamation. Every president since then has followed suit.

My mother raised eight children and deserves a medal tucked into her flowers. As you may have heard, ministers' children are notoriously naughty. But then, we turned out okay (I think). It has become traditional in the U.S. to take Mom out for Sunday dinner, with everybody appropriately decked out in red carnations.

▪ MILDRED SCHULZ'S RHUBARB PIE ▪

Since there is no particular food connected with Mother's Day, I am printing my mother's recipe for rhubarb pie. It is appropriate for the season and is a great gift for every young mother's recipe file. So in honor of all mothers everywhere, and particularly those who cook, Thanks Mom.

PASTRY

2 cups all-purpose flour

1/2 teaspoon sugar

1/4 teaspoon salt

1/2 cup (1 stick) unsalted butter, chilled

3 tablespoons vegetable shortening, chilled

4 to 5 tablespoons orange juice or cold water

FILLING

2 1/2 cups cubed fresh rhubarb (about 2 medium ribs)

3 tablespoons all-purpose flour

1/2 teaspoon ground cinnamon

1/8 teaspoon salt

1/4 teaspoon finely grated lemon peel

1/4 teaspoon finely grated orange peel

1 1/4 cups plus 1 tablespoon sugar

3 tablespoons unsalted butter, melted

3 large eggs, lightly beaten

1. *To make the pastry:* In a medium bowl, combine the flour with the sugar and salt. Cut in the butter and shortening with a knife. Blend with a pastry blender until the mixture has the texture of coarse crumbs. Add the juice, about a tablespoon at a time, and mix gently with a fork or your fingertips to form a soft dough. Do not overwork. Refrigerate, covered, for 1 hour.

2. Preheat the oven to 400° F.

3. Roll out slightly more than half the pastry on a lightly floured board. Line a deep 9-inch or regular 10-inch glass or ceramic pie plate with the pastry. Line the pastry with foil and weight it with rice or beans. Bake for 10 minutes. Remove the foil and cool.

4. *To make the filling:* In a large bowl, combine the rhubarb with the flour. Stir in the cinnamon, salt, lemon peel, orange peel, 1 1/4 cups sugar, and melted butter. Mix well and pour into the prebaked pie shell. Pour the beaten eggs evenly over the top.

5. Roll out the remaining pastry and cut it into strips. Place them over the pie in a lattice pattern. Trim and flute the edges. Sprinkle the top of the pie with the remaining 1 tablespoon sugar. Place the pie on a foil-lined baking sheet and bake for 15 minutes. Reduce the oven temperature to 350° F and bake until the crust is golden and the rhubarb is tender, about 45 minutes longer. Cool on a rack.

SERVES 8

✳

CALIFORNIA STRAWBERRY FESTIVAL— THIRD WEEKEND IN MAY

OXNARD, CALIFORNIA, calls itself the "Strawberry Capital of the World." And when the strawberry crop is ripe and at its juicy best, the town holds a party to celebrate, featuring clowns, magicians, arts and crafts, and a petting zoo. The food is "gourmet" and the strawberry, needless to say, takes center stage. There is a Strawberryland for the kids, in case they get a little bored, but most important, there is, for the grown-ups, a "Berry-Off" cooking contest and (my favorite) a build-it-yourself shortcake stand where you start with a slab of pound cake and pile on all the strawberries and whipped cream you can manage. The festival would not be complete without the search for the perfect Miss Strawberry Blonde, and in case you're wondering, your hair need not be "natural"—or even your own for that matter (wigs are allowed). For more information, contact the Oxnard Special Events Office at (805) 385-7457.

California Strawberry Festival

GRANDMA KJELDSEN'S
■ NORWEGIAN STRAWBERRY SHORTCAKE ■

This recipe comes to me via an associate, Linda Holland Rathkopf, who happens to be one very talented artist. She also happens to be a very good cook and got this recipe from Susan Roos, a teacher at her son Jordan's school. The recipe was passed down to Susan from her grandmother. Even fourth hand, or perhaps because it is, this is a wonderful, and unusual, recipe for shortcake.

½ cup (1 stick) unsalted butter, at room
   temperature
1½ cups sugar
4 eggs, separated
1 cup all-purpose flour
1 teaspoon vanilla extract

1 tablespoon baking powder
½ cup milk
1 pint heavy cream
1 pint medium strawberries, cleaned
   and hulled

1. Preheat oven to 325° F. Lightly grease two 8-inch-square cake pans.

2. Beat the butter and ½ cup of the sugar in a large mixing bowl until light and smooth. Add the egg yolks one at a time, beating well after each addition. Add the flour, vanilla, baking powder, and milk; continue beating until batter is smooth. Batter will be quite thick. Spoon evenly into the prepared pans.

3. Beat the egg whites with remaining 1 cup sugar in a large bowl until stiff but not dry. Spread over top of batter in pans. Bake for 20 minutes, or until top is firm and golden brown. Turn the oven off and let the cakes cool in the oven for 25 minutes. Place them on a rack until completely cooled.

4. Unmold the cakes with a spatula. Place one on a serving dish.

5. Beat the cream in a large bowl until stiff peaks form. Spread a layer of cream over the first cake. Add half the strawberries. Top with the second cake. Spread evenly with the remaining whipped cream and remaining strawberries. Refrigerate until ready to serve.

SERVES 8

ONE OF SPRING'S culinary delights is the fiddlehead fern—actually the top of a type of fern that hasn't unfolded yet, giving it the appearance of the musical instrument. For those who may have never had the pleasure of tasting this treat, take a drive to Monroe, Maine—about 2½ hours north of Portland—which hosts an annual fiddlehead festival.

One rarely sees so many fiddleheads in one place, and certainly one never finds elsewhere the range of dishes that the fiddleheads lend their stamp to—from doughnuts to ravioli to quiche. For more information, contact the Maine Trappers at (207) 525-3588.

■ FIDDLEHEAD FESTIVAL'S ■ FIDDLEHEAD QUICHE

This recipe, origin unknown, is included in the Fiddlehead Festival's official publication. Use your favorite pie pastry or the one on page 71. To prepare fiddleheads, trim any brown pieces off the ferns and swish them in water to clean. Cook in a small amount of boiling salted water until tender, about 10 minutes.

Pastry for a 9- to 10-inch pie
4 eggs
1 cup heavy cream
2 tablespoons finely chopped onion
½ teaspoon salt
¼ teaspoon freshly ground pepper

Pinch cayenne
1¼ cups shredded Swiss or Jarlsberg
   cheese
2 slices crisp-fried bacon, crumbled
1½ cups cooked fiddleheads

1. Preheat the oven to 400° F. Roll out the pastry and line a 9- or 10-inch pie plate. Trim and flute the edges. Prick with a fork and bake for 6 minutes, or until lightly browned. Cool. Reduce the oven temperature to 375° F.

2. In a medium bowl, mix the eggs with the cream, onion, salt, pepper, and cayenne.

3. Sprinkle half the cheese over the bottom of the crust. Sprinkle the bacon over the cheese and top with half the fiddleheads. Pour in the egg mixture and add the remaining cheese and then the remaining fiddleheads. Bake until a knife inserted in the center comes out clean, about 30 minutes. Let stand for 10 minutes before serving.

SERVES 6 TO 8

✳

MEMORIAL DAY—
LAST MONDAY IN MAY

MEMORIAL DAY, originally known as Decoration Day, came into being after the end of the Civil War. It is said that in 1863, in Columbus, Mississippi, the women of the town decorated the graves of both Union and Confederate soldiers with flowers. In 1868 the Grand Army of the Republic designated May 30 for that purpose. At that first "official" celebration at Arlington, Virginia, General James A. Garfield, congressman, future president, and brilliant orator, said in part, "If silence is ever golden, it must be here beside the graves of fifteen thousand men whose lives were more significant than speech and whose death was a poem the music of which can never be sung . . ." Memorial Day gradually became a day on which to remember all of our nation's war heroes.

Memorial Day is a holiday that grew out of spontaneity. Unfortunately, that spontaneity, along with the true meaning of the holiday, has been almost totally lost. Instead, the holiday now signals the end of spring and the beginning of the summer season. The great stock-car race at Indianapolis, the Indianapolis 500, is the significant event of the weekend and dominates the news. In my family we used to listen to the race on the radio, though for the life of me, I can't imagine why, particularly since we had our own race to watch—the race up Lookout Mountain in Golden, Colorado, which we could watch from our front porch. It was a race against the clock—the road was too narrow to permit any other kind. One car at a time sped up the road through its hairpin loops and turns. Not all of them made it. Finally, after one too many crashes, the race was brought to a halt once and for all. Car crashes notwithstanding, those were good days, and good days are meant to be shared with family—particularly over a good meal.

⚜

▪ MIXED GRILL WITH CHIMICHURRI SAUCE ▪

*M*emorial Day is the weekend when most of us pull out our grills from the garage and clean them up. Though it is not technically summer yet, the three-day holiday gets us in the mood for the season ahead. And since this is most likely our first outdoor meal of the year, it's nice to make it into a special occasion.

In Argentina, where barbecue is synonymous with socializing, a mixed grill includes chicken, beef, and sausage. The heady chimichurri (hot chile) marinade used for basting during cooking, and dipping later, is often dubbed "the sauce of life."

CHIMICHURRI MARINADE
½ cup vegetable oil
½ cup malt vinegar
¼ cup water
2 tablespoons chopped fresh parsley
3 large cloves garlic, minced
1 teaspoon cayenne
1 teaspoon salt
1½ teaspoons chopped fresh oregano
½ teaspoon freshly ground pepper

MIXED GRILL
1 chicken (about 3 pounds), cut into pieces
1 pound sirloin beef, cut into 1¼-inch cubes
6 sweet Italian sausages
Vegetable oil

1. Combine all of the marinade ingredients in a glass jar with a tight-fitting lid. Let stand at room temperature for 24 hours.

2. Place the chicken pieces in a shallow glass or ceramic dish; coat them lightly with the marinade. Refrigerate, covered, for 3 hours.

3. Place the beef cubes and sausages in separate shallow glass or ceramic dishes; coat them lightly with the marinade. Refrigerate, covered, for 1 hour.

4. Remove the chicken and meat from the refrigerator. Heat the grill.

5. If using a charcoal grill, bank the coals on one end of the coal grate; place the drip pan on the other end. If using presoaked wood chips or chunks, sprinkle them

over the hot coals. If using a gas grill, place the drip pan on one side of the grill, directly on the lava rocks, and add any presoaked chips to the pan. Brush the grid lightly with oil.

6. Place the dark meat over the direct heat and cook, covered and with the vents open, basting with extra sauce and turning once, for 15 minutes. Add the white meat and cook, covered, for 5 minutes. Place the sausages over the drip pan and continue to cook, covered, basting and turning the chicken once, for 10 minutes.

7. Meanwhile, thread the beef cubes on skewers.

8. Remove the drip pan from the grill and stir up the coals, knocking off the gray ash if using charcoal. Place the beef cubes and sausages over the hottest part of the coals, and move the chicken pieces to the cooler edges. Grill the sausages and beef cubes, turning often, until done, about 15 minutes. Serve on a platter with individual bowls of the remaining sauce.

SERVES 4 TO 6

✳

KODIAK CRAB FESTIVAL — MEMORIAL DAY WEEKEND

THIS FESTIVAL is held on Kodiak Island, Alaska, to celebrate the end of crab season. Needless to say, how the year has gone for the crabbers determines how the festival goes for everyone (usually, just great, thanks). Aside from the typical games, parades, balls, and rides on the fairway that accompany such festivals, there are contests galore. And though the food at the booths is varied and international, those booths that feature crab dishes are the real draw. Alaskan waters are known for three kinds of crabs: Dungeness, snow, and king. For the most part, Alaskan crabs are interchangeable. The king crab legs, tinged with red, are probably the most recognizable. The snow crab is usually sold in crab meat form. The Dungeness, highly regarded for its flavor, is usually sold whole, fresh or frozen. For more information, contact the Kodiak Area Chamber of Commerce at (907) 486-5557.

■ KING CRAB ROYALE ■

*T*he following recipe uses king crab legs and comes to us courtesy of the Alaska Seafood Marketing Institute. The crab may be prepared under the broiler or on a grill—which makes it a great springtime recipe.

12 ounces split Alaska king crab legs,
   thawed if necessary
1/4 cup (1/2 stick) unsalted butter, melted
1 tablespoon lemon juice
2 teaspoons grated onion
1 clove garlic, crushed

1 tablespoon finely chopped fresh
   parsley
1/4 teaspoon dried tarragon leaves,
   crushed
Dash hot pepper sauce

1. Cut the crab legs into 3-inch pieces. If desired, remove the crabmeat from the shells and cut it into bite-sized pieces for easier serving; return to shells. Combine the remaining ingredients and brush over the crab.

2. Broil shell side down, about 4 inches from the flame, brushing once or twice with the remaining sauce, for about 4 minutes. Or grill, shell side down, over hot coals, brushing once or twice with the remaining sauce, for about 5 minutes.

SERVES 2 AS A MAIN COURSE, 4 AS AN APPETIZER

SUMMER RECIPES

Jeff Davis Pie

Apricot-Walnut Muffins

Butter-Pecan Turtles

Grilled Butterflied Leg of Lamb

Fried Fish Sandwich

Grilled Shrimp and Sausages on Red, Red Rice

Carob-Chip Cookies

Baked Cranberry Beans

Old-Fashioned Potato Salad

Cherry Triangles

Nutty Wild-Rice Pancakes

Cream of Black-Eyed Pea Soup

Steamed Soft-Shell Clams

Fried Onion Rings

Roasted Garlic and Leek Chowder

White Bean Soup

Lobster—Boiled, Steamed, or Broiled

Green Tomato Stew

Fried Watermelon Rinds

Zucchini Muffin Gems

Blueberry Muffins

❋

SUMMER

✳

WHEN I THINK of summertime, the images that come to mind are of kids running around food-laden blankets spread out on Central Park's Great Lawn, and young folks partying around roaring bonfires on the beaches of Long Island's Amagansett and East Hampton—places where I have spent many summers, enjoying the sheer pleasure of dining al fresco. I have also had a few memorable picnics on the banks of the Hudson River, the majesty of that mighty waterway making the food almost an afterthought.

I was not raised in a family that packed hampers and made summertime excursions to the country for the luxury of eating in wide-open spaces. Partially, I suppose, because Mom and Dad just had too many young ones to feed (there were eight of us), but also because, weather permitting, we generally ate outdoors anyway, on the patio outside the kitchen door. We didn't eat barbecue, either. My dad rarely used the grill. Rather, we just moved the normal, everyday inside meal, lock, stock, and barrel, outside. My mom served one-dish dinners with names like "Russian Hamburger" (meat sauce with peas over rice), "Firehouses" (meatballs with carrots served on potatoes), and "Shipwreck" (potatoes, ground meat, and kidney beans)— meals I remember fondly to this day.

My favorite outdoor meals, however, were those shared with my brother on nearby Table Mountain, which to us was just an extension of our backyard. The two of us spent many happy hours on the mountain and often took our lunch with us. Two years my senior, Tommy had been struck by polio before I was born and opted to have his withered leg amputated by the time he was thirteen. He was my equal in most things, and my better in the rest, and we were very close. To his credit, and my constant pride, Tom's affliction never stopped him. He could do more on crutches than most people could with two legs. He and I loved that mountain. We even had our secret hideouts. One, a shallow cave in the cliff tops, gave a splendid view of our town below. Another, a giant boulder shaded by a single aspen tree, provided a natural terraced eating spot.

Our lunch was packed in paper bags (my preference: peanut butter and iceberg lettuce on Wonder bread). We took turns carrying a thermos of Kool-Aid up the mountain. Where, perhaps due to thin air, or just our overactive imaginations, we shut out the world and roamed the bluffs; vicariously living the adventures of Tom Swift, the Hardy Boys, and Gene Autry and his underground city.

The big open-air eating event of those summers was our church picnic. Once a year my father, then the pastor at St. James Lutheran Church in Golden, Colorado, delivered his sermon high in the Rockies, his words echoing like a John Denver melody around the valley where these gatherings took place. The food, brought by parishioners, was always plentiful. The picnic invariably ended with a dazzling array of desserts: cakes, cookies, pies, and sometimes turnovers and cobblers. But the best part for me, other than the endless supply of soda pop, was that moment at dusk, after refuse fires were lit, when the giant containers of ice cream were rolled out and cones were scooped out for everyone, young and old alike.

❅

■ JUNE ■

It is the month of June,
The month of leaves and roses,
When pleasant sights salute our eyes
And pleasant scents the noses.

—NATHANIEL PARKER WILLIS,
"THE MONTH OF JUNE"

Though there are quite a few theories about the origin of the word *June*, a popular one is that it derives from Juno, the goddess and patroness of women. Her name was also invoked for marriage and childbirth, which explains the desire of most women to be "June brides." June also contains the summer solstice (about the 22nd)—the longest day of the year.

❋

■ JUNE SPECIAL EVENTS ■

NATIONAL DAIRY MONTH: Sponsored by the American Dairy Association to honor America's dairy farmers and their products.

JUNE IS TURKEY LOVERS' MONTH: Sponsored by the National Turkey Federation to get people to eat more turkey all year round. For recipes and more information, call (703) 435-7209.

NATIONAL FRESH FRUIT AND VEGETABLE MONTH: Sponsored by the United Fresh Fruit and Vegetable Association to promote the goodness (good taste, good nutrition, good value) of fresh produce.

NATIONAL PAPAYA MONTH: The Hawaiian papaya season reaches its peak during June—hence the promotion, sponsored by the Papaya Administration committee in Honolulu to tout the fruit's taste and nutritional values.

*

JEFFERSON DAVIS'S BIRTHDAY — JUNE 3

JEFFERSON DAVIS, born on this day in 1808, was the first and only president of the Confederate States of America (1861–65). Davis, of Welsh descent, entered college at the age of thirteen and was appointed to the Military Academy at West Point at the age of sixteen. He graduated in 1828. After serving in the army, he returned home to Mississippi (he moved there as a small boy from Kentucky, where he was born) with his new bride, who died shortly thereafter. Davis was devastated and remained single for ten years. He remarried in 1845, the same year he was elected to the House of Representatives. Davis resigned from Congress in 1846 to participate in the Mexican War. In 1847 he reentered politics and was sent to the U.S. Senate by the citizens of Mississippi. He would resign several more times over the years, most notably because of his proslavery stance. He did, however, go on to serve as Secretary of War under Franklin Pierce and was instrumental in the Gadsden Purchase. In 1861, a senator once again, Davis resigned for the last time when the southern states decided to secede. He immediately became the commander of the troops for Mississippi, but at the convention of the seceding states, he was elected president of the Confederacy. He was eventually captured in Georgia in 1865 and thrown in jail without trial. Two years later, still without trial, he was released from jail. He was allowed to stay in the country but was stripped of his citizenship and deprived of all rights. He had lost everything in the war, and it was only due to the generosity of a benefactor that he had a place to live until he died in 1889.

His birthday was first celebrated as a legal holiday in Florida in 1892. Other southern states soon followed. His citizenship was restored posthumously in 1978 by President Carter, who declared that it was "time to end the enmities and recriminations of the past." His birthday is observed by some states on the first Monday of the month.

▪ JEFF DAVIS PIE ▪

*J*eff Davis Pie is the traditional dessert served in the South on this day. There are countless variations of this pie, which is basically a sugar-and-custard affair. Some say it must be made with brown sugar and contain dates and raisins; others insist that it be kept pure and smooth as custard. Then, too, if you add lemon juice, as some versions do, you come close to chess pie, another Southern favorite. The following uses brown sugar. If you think it is too sweet, reduce the amount as you see fit. If you'd like to add dates and raisins, feel free, but dust them lightly with flour first so they don't automatically sink to the bottom.

PASTRY

1¼ cups all-purpose flour

Pinch salt

4 tablespoons (¼ stick) cold unsalted butter

4 tablespoons cold vegetable shortening

2 tablespoons cold water or orange juice

FILLING

1 cup (packed) dark brown sugar

2 tablespoons all-purpose flour

1 teaspoon cinnamon

½ teaspoon nutmeg

1 cup heavy cream

4 eggs, lightly beaten

¼ cup (½ stick) unsalted butter, melted

1. *To make the pastry:* Combine the flour with the salt in a medium bowl. Cut in the butter and shortening with a knife. Blend with a pastry blender until the mixture has the texture of coarse crumbs. Add the water, a tablespoon at a time, and mix gently with a fork to form a soft dough. Do not overwork. Refrigerate for 1 hour.

2. Preheat the oven to 350° F. Roll out the pastry and line a 10-inch glass or ceramic quiche dish. Trim and flute the edges.

3. *To make the filling:* Combine the sugar with the flour, cinnamon, and nutmeg in a medium bowl. Stir in the cream, eggs, and butter.

4. Pour the filling into a prepared pie shell. Bake in center of oven until a knife inserted in center comes out clean, about 50 minutes. Cool on a rack. Serve at room temperature or slightly chilled, cut into thin slices.

SERVES 8 TO 10

PATTERSON, CALIFORNIA, calls itself the "Apricot Capital of the World." The town, located about twenty miles southwest of Modesto in the San Joaquin Valley, has been sponsoring this apricot festival, which features parades, cooking contests, and the like, for over twenty years. More than one hundred craftsmen participate in this event, with upwards of thirty food vendors selling goodies of all kinds. The fiesta is actually held right *before* the local harvest begins. One reason for this is that high school is still in session, which makes the band available for the parade. Also, as the fruit begins to reach its peak, all hands are needed to get in the crop. This is not to say you won't find any fresh apricots at the fiesta; you will—just not bushel after bushel of them. You will also be able to try them in pies, tarts, ice cream, and other goodies. And don't forget to take some dried apricots home. Dried apricots now account for 26 percent of the market—and that number is growing. For more information, contact the Patterson Apricot Fiesta at (209) 892-3118.

■ APRICOT-WALNUT MUFFINS ■

The following recipe uses dried apricots, most of which are sun-dried for three days before being packed and shipped. These muffins are on the tart side, so add more sugar, or some honey, if your tooth is decidedly sweet.

1½ cups sifted all-purpose flour	½ cup finely chopped dried apricots
2 teaspoons baking powder	½ cup chopped walnuts
½ teaspoon salt	1 egg, lightly beaten
Pinch freshly grated nutmeg	1 cup milk
½ cup sugar	¼ cup vegetable oil

1. Preheat the oven to 425° F. Grease a 12-cup muffin tin that has 2½-inch cups.

2. In a large bowl, sift the flour with the baking powder, salt, nutmeg, and sugar. Stir in the apricots and walnuts.

3. In a separate bowl, combine the egg, milk, and oil. Stir into the flour mixture; do not overmix. Fill each cup about seven-eighths full. Bake until golden and firm to the touch, about 25 minutes.

MAKES 12 LARGE MUFFINS

THIS EVENT has been held for close to forty years in Enosburg Falls, north of Montpelier, and it is the largest festival in the state of Vermont. The weekend is packed with lively events, including several long-distance runs, milking contests, greased-pig wrestling, a horse-pulling competition, bathtub races, a parade, and a baking contest. There are farm-related hands-on learning activities as well. If you have never milked a cow, here's your chance. If you go on Saturday, don't miss the chicken barbecue—it's famous in this neck of the woods. For more information, contact the Vermont Dairy Festival at (802) 933-2513

▪ BUTTER-PECAN TURTLES ▪

These bar cookies, which my sister, Jeanette Deschamps, sent one wonderful Christmas some time ago, are one of the best uses of dairy (read butter) *that I know.*

2 cups all-purpose flour
1½ cups light brown sugar, packed
18½ tablespoons (2 sticks plus 2½ tablespoons) unsalted butter, softened

1 cup pecan halves
One 5-ounce bar milk chocolate, cut into bits

1. Preheat the oven to 350° F.

2. In the large bowl of an electric mixer, combine the flour with 1 cup brown sugar and 8 tablespoons (1 stick) butter. Beat until smooth. Spread the mixture over the bottom of an ungreased 10 x 13-inch pan. Spread the pecan halves over the top.

3. Combine the remaining 10½ tablespoons butter and remaining ½ cup brown sugar in a small saucepan. Heat to boiling, stirring constantly. Boil for 1 minute while continuing to stir. Pour evenly over the crust. Bake until the caramel layer is bubbly and the crust is golden, about 20 minutes.

4. Remove from the oven and immediately sprinkle the surface with chocolate bits. Allow the chocolate to melt slightly. Using the point of a knife, gently swirl the chocolate as the pieces melt (do not spread). Cool completely before cutting into 1½-inch squares.

MAKES ABOUT 4½ DOZEN

SEVERAL BASQUE FESTIVALS are held in the state of Nevada, where many Basque sheepherders, fleeing political upheavals in their homeland at the turn of the century, settled. They were welcomed with open arms out West by sheep granges because of their shepherding skills. They were welcomed with rifles by ranchers. Ah, the Old West. The festival in Winnemucca, at the foot of Sonoma Peak, features a parade, games of strength, sheep and hog herding, and folk dancing. The food is "Basque barbecue." That's mutton, in case you're wondering. For more information, contact the Humboldt County Chamber of Commerce at (702) 623-2225. (For information on the Basque festival in Ely, call (702) 289-8877. For Reno festivals, call 800-FOR-RENO.)

▪ GRILLED BUTTERFLIED LEG OF LAMB ▪

It's hard to find mutton in most parts of America. But then, most Americans aren't inclined to look for it because of its reputation for gaminess. Lamb, however, is another matter completely. Buttermilk is commonly used as a marinade for lamb out West, though thinned yogurt, which Californians seem to dote on, is also excellent.

1 leg of lamb (5 to 6 pounds), boned and butterflied	2 sprigs fresh rosemary
	½ teaspoon hot red pepper flakes
2 cloves garlic, minced	2 cups buttermilk

1. Place the lamb in a shallow glass or ceramic dish. Add the garlic and rosemary sprigs to the dish. Sprinkle the lamb with the hot pepper flakes. Pour the buttermilk over the lamb. Refrigerate, covered, overnight. Remove from the refrigerator at least 30 minutes before grilling.

2. Grill the lamb, covered, with all vents open, over medium-hot coals for 12 minutes per side for rare, 15 minutes per side for medium-rare. Let it stand for 10 minutes before serving.

SERVES 6 TO 8

FESTIVAL OF THE FISH —
THIRD WEEKEND IN JUNE

THROUGHOUT THE MIDWEST, the Friday-night fish fry at the local eatery has long been a popular way to spend a pleasant evening. You can find fish fries on menus in the oddest of places—I partook of my first fish fry at the airport restaurant in Wausau, Wisconsin. But the most fun fries are those that are part of a festival and take place out of doors, usually on the banks of a lake. One such event is the Festival of the Fish, held on the shores of Lake Erie in the quaint fishing village of Vermillion, Ohio. Numerous activities take place throughout this historic village—a boat show, a parade, a beauty pageant, games, contests, etc.—but the real reason to go is to eat fried fish. It can be enjoyed on thick-crusted bread in sandwich form, or as part of a fish dinner, which generally includes French fries and a vegetable. (If you go far enough south, you'll get hush puppies instead.) For more information, contact the Vermillion Chamber of Commerce at (216) 967-4477.

▪ FRIED FISH SANDWICH ▪

*M*ost fish-fry masters use a beer batter for dipping the fish and deep frying (for beer batter, see page 93). However, for an easy-to-prepare home recipe, try the following.

⅓ cup all-purpose flour

½ teaspoon salt

⅛ teaspoon freshly ground pepper

1 egg

1 tablespoon dry white wine or
  vermouth

¾ to 1 cup cracker crumbs or fine bread
  crumbs

4 flounder fillets (about 10 ounces each)

2 tablespoons unsalted butter

2 tablespoons olive oil

1 tablespoon chopped fresh chives

4 rolls, split and buttered

1. Combine the flour with the salt and pepper on a plate. In a shallow bowl, beat the egg with the wine. Place the cracker crumbs on another plate. Dust the fish lightly with flour. Dip in the egg mixture and coat lightly with crumbs.

2. Heat the butter and oil in a large heavy skillet over medium heat. Sauté the fish until it is golden and flakes when tested with a fork, about 3 minutes on each side. Sprinkle with chives. Place each fillet on a roll.

SERVES 4

FATHER'S DAY—
THIRD SUNDAY IN JUNE

AS EARLY AS 1924, there was a big movement afoot in this country to set aside a day on which we honored dads. Calvin Coolidge was a strong supporter of the idea. But *he* didn't sign it into law—Richard Nixon finally did in 1972, making Father's Day a national holiday, on a par with Mother's Day.

In the last twenty years, gift giving has become a tradition on Father's Day. And ties, even though we joke about them, are still perhaps the most popular gifts. Other hot items include virtually anything that has to do with an outdoor grill—wood-handled utensils, mitts, grills themselves, and even barbecue cookbooks. After all, it is that time of year. When my book *Cooking with Fire & Smoke* was published in 1986, I was asked to do a guest segment on the "Hour Magazine" television show. The theme was Father's Day, and I was asked to demonstrate my expertise at outdoor cooking and share my knowledge of equipment any dad would be very happy to receive. There was one slight hitch: I couldn't actually light a grill on the set, as it would set off all the fire alarms in the studio. But through the magic of television and the behind-the-scenes genius of Chris Circosta who fired up *his* grill sitting outside the studio's fire doors, everything worked just fine. Even though there was no sizzle on the gas grill, the shrimp and sausages were grilled to perfection.

▪ GRILLED SHRIMP AND SAUSAGES
ON RED, RED RICE ▪

This is the dish I prepared (or rather, Chris prepared and I finished) for the Father's Day tribute on "Hour Magazine." (Cooking with Fire & Smoke, incidentally, has been published in paperback by Fireside and is still available.)

Red, Red Rice (recipe follows)
16 large shrimp, shelled and deveined
3 tablespoons olive oil
2 tablespoons chopped fresh basil

½ teaspoon freshly ground pepper
1½ cups dry white wine
1½ pounds hot Italian sausage

1. Prepare the Red, Red Rice through step 3. Set aside.

2. Place the shrimp in a glass or ceramic bowl. Add the oil, basil, and pepper. Toss well. Cover and let stand for 30 minutes.

3. In a saucepan big enough to hold the sausages in a single layer, heat the wine to boiling. Reduce the heat. Prick the sausages and gently poach them in the wine for 3 minutes per side. Drain.

4. Preheat a grill.

5. Finish the rice; keep it warm in a low oven. Prick the sausages once more and thread the shrimp onto skewers.

6. Place the sausages on an oiled grid and cook, covered, over hot coals for 5 minutes. Remove the cover, turn the sausages, and cook for 3 minutes. Add the shrimp to the grill. Grill the shrimp for 5 minutes, turning once. To serve, place a mound of rice on a plate. Place a sausage in the middle and top with four shrimp.

SERVES 4

RED, RED RICE

1 cup long-grain rice
1 large red bell pepper
3 tablespoons unsalted butter
1 teaspoon olive oil

¼ cup thinly sliced scallion, white parts
   only
Salt and freshly ground pepper

1. Bring a large pot of salted water to a boil. Add the rice. Stir while the water returns to a boil; boil for 12 minutes. Drain the rice into a colander. Place the colander over steaming water and cover the rice with one sheet of paper towel. Steam for 15 minutes.

2. Meanwhile, char the pepper over a gas flame, under a broiler, or on a grill. Wrap the charred pepper in paper towels and place in a plastic bag. Cool for 5 minutes. Rub off the charred skin with paper towels. Seed the pepper and roughly chop.

3. In a large skillet over medium heat, heat 2 tablespoons of butter and the oil. Add the scallion; cook for 2 minutes. Do not brown. Add the chopped pepper and cook for 1 minute. Transfer the mixture to a food processor; process until smooth.

4. Add the rice to the same skillet with the remaining tablespoon of butter. Add the processed pepper mixture and toss until well mixed. (The rice will take on a red hue.) Add salt and pepper to taste. Keep warm in a low oven until ready to serve.

SERVES 4

❄

SUMMER SOLSTICE—ON OR ABOUT JUNE 22

The summer solstice occurs about June 22, when the sun is at the north-ernmost point of its elliptic orbit. From this point until the autumnal equinox in the Northern Hemisphere, the days shorten, until, with the arrival of autumn (about September 22), day and night are once again of equal length.

✳

ST. JOHN'S (MIDSUMMER'S) DAY—
JUNE 24

THE FEAST of St. John the Baptist is said to be one of the oldest feast days in honor of any saint. The exact date of his birth is not known, but it *is* accepted that he was born about six months before Jesus. (John and Jesus were related. John's mother, Elizabeth, was Mary's cousin.) John would go out into the wilderness beyond Jordan and preach repentance and perform baptisms. He proclaimed the coming of Jesus and would, in fact, baptize him. John was eventually imprisoned for speaking out against Herod (Antipas) and Herodias's daughter, Salome (speaking on her mother's behalf), asked for John's head on a dish.

St. John's birthday happens to coincide with the summer solstice—yet another example of a religious rite occurring on a pagan holiday. It has often been said that when John preached about the coming of Christ, he stated that "He must increase while I decrease"—a supposed reference to the fact that after John's death, the days become shorter, and after the birth of Christ (Christmas, the winter solstice), the days begin to lengthen.

■ CAROB-CHIP COOKIES ■

It is said that John survived in the wilderness by eating locust beans, the pods of a certain kind of locust tree. The pods (actually the pulp inside them), having given John sustenance, came to be called St. John's bread. We know the same pod as "carob," a popular substitute for chocolate. It tastes similar to chocolate and is most often used in candies. Carob contains no caffeine and doesn't cause the allergic reactions that chocolate can. Nowadays it is easy to find and is even made in chocolate-chip form.

1½ cups plus 2 tablespoons all-purpose
   flour
½ teaspoon baking soda
¼ teaspoon salt
½ cup vegetable shortening
6 tablespoons granulated sugar

6 tablespoons light brown sugar
½ teaspoon vanilla extract
¼ cup milk
1 large egg
6 ounces (about 1 cup) carob chips
½ cup chopped nuts

1. Preheat the oven to 350° F.

2. Sift the flour with the baking soda and salt into a mixing bowl.

3. In a large bowl, beat the shortening with both sugars until creamy. Beat in the vanilla, milk, and egg. Stir in the flour mixture; mix thoroughly. Stir in the carob chips and nuts.

4. Drop the batter by tablespoonfuls onto greased cookie sheets. Bake for 10 minutes, or until edges are lightly browned. Cool on the baking sheets for a few minutes before transferring to a wire rack to cool completely.

MAKES ABOUT 24 COOKIES

■ JULY ■

Yellow butterflies
Over the blossoming virgin corn,
With pollen painted faces
Chase one another in brilliant throng.

—HOPI SONG, *THE OLD FARMER'S*
ALMANAC (1992)

July was originally known as *Quintilis,* meaning "fifth," as it was the fifth month of the year on the Roman calendar. The name was changed by Caesar, in his own honor, to *Julius.* The change, ironically, went into effect in 44 B.C.—the year Caesar was assassinated.

❋

■ JULY—SPECIAL EVENTS ■

JULY BELONGS TO BLUEBERRIES MONTH: Sponsored by the North American Blueberry Council to make everyone aware that this is the peak of the blueberry season.

NATIONAL HOT DOG MONTH: Sponsored by the National Hot Dog and Sausage Council to promote all manner of "dogs" and their versatility —on or off a grill.

NATIONAL ICE CREAM MONTH: Sponsored by the International Ice Cream Association to celebrate America's favorite summertime dessert.

NATIONAL PICNIC MONTH: Sponsored by Campbell's in celebration of classic picnic foods (like baked beans).

INDEPENDENCE DAY — JULY 4

ON JULY 4, 1776, after all the colonies except New York voiced approval, John Hancock, president of the Continental Congress, and Charles Thomson, secretary, signed the first copy of the Declaration of Independence (though it would take some time before representatives from all thirteen colonies—including New York—actually signed the document).

The first official Independence Day, or Fourth of July, was observed in Philadelphia in 1777. The windows of every house in the city were lit with candles. Ships in the harbor fired a thirteen-gun salute. The Fourth of July quickly became the foremost patriotic holiday of our fledgling country. It still is, of course, and it's quite a day for fireworks.

I love fireworks. When I was growing up, the town of Golden, Colorado, set off its fireworks from the top of Castle Rock. It was great for our family—we didn't have to move an inch to see them. It was wonderful to see the fountains of glittering, shimmering sparkles lighting up the cliffs. One year lives forever in my memory. We were still settling down in our front yard as the fireworks began. Suddenly, there was a torrent of rockets, sparkles, and bangers that lit up the sky and the mountain as the whole supply of fireworks accidentally ignited en masse into one fantastic show that lasted all of five minutes.

The Fourth of July is a day for being with friends and family, a day to be outdoors —either barbecuing in the backyard or picnicking in the park. The fare need not be fancy. As far as I'm concerned, nothing tastes better than hot dogs and hamburgers cooked on the grill and served with potato salad and baked beans.

▪ BAKED CRANBERRY BEANS ▪

Cranberry beans are often overlooked because people aren't quite sure what to do with them. The small, mottled pink beans are sweet and incredibly flavorsome. They don't need a lot of "fixings," as you can see by this simple recipe.

1 pound dry cranberry beans	4 teaspoons Dijon mustard
1 pound sausage meat	3 tablespoons honey
1 large onion, finely chopped	1½ cups chicken or vegetable stock
2 large cloves garlic, minced	

1. Soak the beans overnight in cold water to cover. Drain.

2. Preheat the oven to 300° F.

3. In a large heavy pot over medium-high heat, sauté the sausage, breaking the meat up into lumps, until well browned. Pour off all but about 3 tablespoons of fat. Reduce the heat to medium.

4. Add the onion to the sausage in the pot; cook for 1 minute. Add the garlic; cook, stirring frequently, for 4 minutes. Stir in the mustard and honey. Stir in 1 cup chicken stock, scraping the sides and bottom of the pot with a wooden spoon. Stir in the drained beans.

5. Transfer the beans to a buttered bean pot or heavy Dutch oven. Cover and bake for 2 hours. Reduce the heat to 275° F and continue to bake, adding additional stock as needed to keep the beans from drying out, until the beans are tender, 1½ to 2 hours.

SERVES 6 TO 8

▪ OLD-FASHIONED POTATO SALAD ▪

The following recipe is simple, but not too simple. The great thing about potato salad is that it is a dish that is open to virtually any interpretation. One can blanket the potatoes with a mayonnaise dressing or douse them with a vinaigrette. The options are limitless. I use a mayonnaise dressing, lightly seasoned with Dijon mustard, paprika, and cayenne pepper.

4 medium baking potatoes
(about 2 pounds)
½ cup finely chopped celery
½ cup chopped dill pickles
4 hard-boiled eggs, peeled and roughly
chopped
1 large clove garlic, minced
½ teaspoon salt

2 teaspoons Dijon mustard
1 teaspoon Hungarian sweet paprika
⅛ teaspoon cayenne
2 tablespoons lemon juice
¼ cup olive oil
⅔ cup mayonnaise
Chopped fresh parsley

1. Cook the potatoes, unpeeled, in boiling water until barely tender, about 20 minutes. Rinse under cold running water and drain. Let cool.

2. Peel the potatoes and cut each in half lengthwise. Cut each half into ¼-inch-thick slices. In a large bowl, combine the potatoes with the celery, pickles, and eggs.

3. In a small bowl, mash the garlic with the salt until a paste is formed. Stir in the mustard, paprika, and cayenne. Whisk in the lemon juice, oil, and mayonnaise. Pour over the potato mixture. Gently toss to mix. Refrigerate, covered, until ready to serve. Sprinkle with parsley before serving.

SERVES 4 TO 6

❋

NATIONAL CHERRY FESTIVAL —
SECOND WEEK IN JULY

TRAVERSE CITY, MICHIGAN, is the "Cherry Capital of the World." The good folks there claim that the region is responsible for 70 percent of the world's red cherry crop. That's a lot of cherries, which is just fine, because this festival draws a lot of visitors. Almost half a million people attend this week-long event, so if you plan to be one of them, it pays to plan ahead. Traverse City sits on the shores of Grand Traverse Bay, and the bay serves as a backdrop for the open-air food market, where you can sample fresh cherries and other goods to your heart's content. There is a cherry cooking contest along with a cherry-wine competition and a pie-eating contest for the kids. The highlight of the week though, is the Friday "smorgasbord," where the cherry is a featured ingredient in every dish. The big attraction for most cherry lovers is the incredible variety of sweets: pies, tarts, cakes, cheesecakes, and just about every other kind of dessert you can think of. For more information, contact the National Cherry Festival at (616) 947-4230.

▪ CHERRY TRIANGLES ▪

Cherry pie is one of my favorite desserts. Another is a pastry my mother, Mildred Schulz, has been making ever since I can remember: cherry-filled triangles of golden dough.

FILLING

3/4 cup sugar

5 tablespoons cornstarch

1/4 teaspoon salt

2 cans (17 ounces each) water-packed
   cherries

1 tablespoon unsalted butter

Few drops red food coloring (optional)

PASTRY

2/3 cup milk, scalded and cooled to
   lukewarm

1 package dry yeast

1 cup (2 sticks) unsalted butter

2 1/2 cups all-purpose flour

4 egg yolks, lightly beaten

ICING

1/4 cup (1/2 stick) unsalted butter

1/2 teaspoon vanilla extract

2 tablespoons heavy cream

1 1/2 cups confectioners' sugar

1. *To make the filling:* In a medium saucepan, combine the sugar with the cornstarch and salt. Drain the cherries, reserving 1 cup of liquid. Whisk the reserved cherry juice into the saucepan. Heat to boiling, reduce the heat, and simmer until the mixture is thick, about 4 minutes. Do not overcook. Add the butter, cherries, and food coloring, if using. Cool, stirring occasionally.

2. Preheat the oven to 350° F.

3. *To make the pastry:* In a small bowl, combine the milk and the yeast. In another bowl, cut the butter into the flour with a knife. Blend with a pastry blender until the mixture has the texture of coarse crumbs. Stir in the milk mixture and the egg yolks. Mix thoroughly.

4. Transfer the dough to a lightly floured board and knead about ten times (turns). Divide the dough in half. Roll out one half to fit an 11 1/2 x 17 1/2-inch jelly-roll pan, and place it in the pan. Spread the cooled cherry mixture over the surface of the dough. Roll out the second half and place it over the top of the cherry filling. Pinch the edges together. Let stand in a warm place for 15 minutes.

5. Bake the pastry on the middle rack of the oven until golden brown and firm to the touch, 45 to 55 minutes. Cool on a rack for 10 minutes.

6. *To make the icing:* In a large bowl, beat the butter with the vanilla and cream. Add the sugar and beat until smooth. Spread over the partially cooled pastry. Cool completely. Cut into 3-inch squares, then cut the squares in half diagonally.

MAKES 48 TRIANGLES

❋

MINNESOTA STATE WILD RICE FESTIVAL—
SECOND WEEKEND IN JULY

THIS FESTIVAL actually takes place on two days in two different northern Minnesota towns. It begins on Saturday in Kelliher, about fifty miles north of Bemidji, the nearest town with motels. The festival includes numerous educational exhibits featuring wild rice, and the first thing you'll probably learn is that wild rice is not rice at all—it's actually a grass that grows in brackish waters.

Wild rice was harvested by Native Americans long before the Europeans came over. It was traditionally picked by women (and still is on Indian reservations), two to a canoe: one navigates the boat through the wild-rice fields while the other shakes and bends the stems until they release the rice. These natural wild-rice areas are protected and can be harvested only by Indians. Nowadays, and off reservation, wild rice is produced in man-made paddies and harvested by huge combines with enormous balloon tires. The growers say that though wild rice has been cultivated, it has not been domesticated. Man-made paddies or not, it is still labeled and sold as wild rice.

Local groups compete by selling baked goods and wild-rice cookbooks. The main event of the day is a beef brisket barbecue with several wild-rice accompaniments. The next morning, the event moves farther north to the town of Waskish, where people flock to the wild-rice pancake breakfast. For more information, contact the Wild Rice Festival at (218) 647-8544.

▪ NUTTY WILD-RICE PANCAKES ▪

*W*hile not the ones that are served in Waskish on Sunday morning, these wild-rice pancakes are excellent with a side of sausage and good maple syrup. These particular pancakes are the handiwork of Jill Gardner of San Francisco.

½ cup all-purpose flour
½ teaspoon baking powder
¼ teaspoon salt
Pinch freshly ground black pepper
½ cup coarsely ground walnuts
1 egg

½ cup sour cream
½ cup milk
1 cup cooked wild rice
4 tablespoons (½ stick) unsalted butter,
  melted

1. In a medium-size bowl, combine the flour, baking powder, salt, pepper, and walnuts. Mix well.

2. In a small bowl, combine the egg, sour cream, and ¼ cup of the milk. Whisk until smooth. Using a wooden spoon, stir into the flour mixture. Let stand for 10 minutes.

3. Stir the remaining ¼ cup milk into the batter. Stir in the cooked wild rice and melted butter.

4. Heat a lightly greased cast-iron skillet or griddle over medium heat until hot but not smoking. Cook the pancakes, a few at a time, using about 3 tablespoons of batter per pancake. When lightly browned (about 2 minutes), turn over and cook on the other side for 1 minute. Transfer to a serving platter and keep warm in a 225° F oven while cooking the remaining pancakes. Reduce the heat under the skillet if the pancakes brown too quickly.

MAKES ABOUT SIXTEEN 2½-INCH TO 3-INCH PANCAKES

❊

EVERY YEAR in the town of Athens, Texas (sixty miles southeast of Dallas), they hold an event that showcases Texas's Southern roots—as opposed to its Southwestern heritage. Black-eyed peas are the stars of the day in this town of 10,000. The festival became popular when the town was booming about twenty years ago and the local pea cannery thrived. The cannery is now gone, but the festival still attracts about 40,000 people annually. If you like black-eyed peas (which are actually beans), you will find them everywhere—in your martini, as well as in an astonishing assortment of foods, ranging from appetizers to desserts. From shellin' and pea poppin' to a "black-eyed pea taste-in," fun is promised to all. What's more, there are lots of booths that sell barbecue of all sorts. For more information, contact the Athens Chamber of Commerce at (214) 675-5181.

▪ CREAM OF BLACK-EYED PEA SOUP ▪

In the South, black-eyed peas are often cooked with ham hocks and greens. They are also the basis of the New Year's dish Hoppin' John (see page 197), and they are good in soup. If you use dried peas, instead of frozen as called for below, cook them for about 3 hours and add more liquid to the pot.

1 tablespoon unsalted butter
1 medium onion, finely chopped
1 small hot green pepper, seeded,
    deveined, and minced
1 cup diced ham
1 package (10 ounces) frozen black-eyed
    peas, defrosted

¼ cup dry white wine
4 cups chicken broth
½ cup heavy cream
Salt and freshly ground pepper
Chopped fresh parsley

1. Melt the butter in a medium saucepan over medium-low heat. Add the onion and hot green pepper. Cook, without browning, for 5 minutes. Stir in the ham and peas. Add the wine and raise the heat. Cook, stirring often, until the wine evaporates. Add the chicken broth. Heat to boiling, reduce the heat, and simmer until the peas are very tender, about 1 hour.

2. Add the cream to the soup and heat, without boiling, until hot. Add salt and pepper to taste. Sprinkle with parsley.

SERVES 4

ADD THE SOFT-SHELL CLAM to Maine's list of incredible seafood. At the Yarmouth Clam Festival in Yarmouth, Maine, these delicacies are served up raw, steamed, or fried. And clams are not the only seafood you can sink your teeth into here. Lobsters, scallops, tuna, and an endless cornucopia of other foods are available as well: Numerous activities are featured over this weekend. Races, demonstrations, parades, concerts, and arts-and-crafts exhibits help draw a crowd of more than 75,000. And you won't want to miss the blueberry-pancake breakfast served on Sunday morning. For more information, contact the Yarmouth Clam Festival at (207) 846-3984.

▪ STEAMED SOFT-SHELL CLAMS ▪

On the East Coast, the most popular soft-shell clam is the steamer; out west, it's the razor clam. This recipe feeds one hungry person for dinner. Reduce the amount if you wish.

18 to 24 soft-shell clams   Unsalted butter, melted
1 tablespoon cornstarch

1. Scrub the clams and soak them for 30 minutes in a large pot of cold water to which you have added the cornstarch. Rinse well.

2. Place 2 inches of cold salted water in a pot and add the clams. Heat to boiling; cook, covered, until the clams open, usually no more than 3 minutes. Discard any unopened clams. Strain the broth and serve the clams with the broth and melted butter.

SERVES 1

✳

WALLA WALLA SWEET ONION FESTIVAL— SECOND SUNDAY IN JULY

ONCE A YEAR, Walla Walla, Washington, plays host to a one-day celebration of its most famous products—onions. Walla Walla onions are legendary for their sweetness, and there are always plenty on hand here for the tasting. This country produces other sweet onions—Vidalia in Georgia, Maui in Hawaii, California Imperials, and Texas Supersweets—but they all come from two varieties: the Grano (large and round or slim and elongated) or the Granex (oval with flattened ends). Walla Walla onions, on the other hand, include a few strains like the French onion, first planted in Walla Walla in 1900 (from seeds shipped from Corsica), and the Arbini, named in honor of its developer, John Arbini. Aside from a recipe contest, the festival features an onion shot put, an onion hunt, an onion-ring toss, an onion-slicing contest, a trivia contest, and more. There are a lot of onion dishes to sample, but fried onion rings are probably the all-time favorites. For more information, contact the Walla Walla Chamber of Commerce at (509) 525-0850.

▪ FRIED ONION RINGS ▪

*T*hese can be made with any yellow onion, but using one of the sweet varieties turns a good dish into a delectable one.

1 cup all-purpose flour
1 tablespoon dry mustard
1 teaspoon freshly grated nutmeg
½ teaspoon salt

4 eggs, separated
1 cup beer
2 pounds sweet onions
Vegetable oil for frying

1. In a medium bowl, combine the flour with the mustard, nutmeg, and salt.

2. In a separate bowl, combine the egg yolks with the beer and whisk until smooth. Add this to the flour mixture and whisk once again until smooth. Refrigerate, covered, for 8 hours.

3. Cut the onions into ¼-inch-thick slices. Place the sliced onions in a large bowl, cover with ice water, and let stand for 15 minutes.

4. Beat the egg whites until stiff and fold them into the batter.

5. Drain the onions, divide the slices into rings, and lightly pat dry with paper towels.

6. Heat 2 inches of oil in a large saucepan until hot but not smoking. Dip the onion rings into the batter, shaking off excess. Fry the rings in the hot oil until golden brown.

SERVES 6 TO 8

✳

GILROY GARLIC FESTIVAL— LAST FULL WEEKEND IN JULY

THE GILROY GARLIC FESTIVAL may be one of the most famous food festivals in the country, if not the world. All the dishes served, from escargot and blackened shrimp to ice cream and peanut butter cups, are flavored with garlic. Gilroy, California, is the garlic center of America. About 90 percent of our garlic grows within a hundred-mile radius of the town. Garlic just hangs in the air. Will Rogers is supposed to have said that Gilroy was "the only place in America where you can marinate a steak by hanging it on the clothesline." Be sure to visit the garlic topping and braiding exhibits, and don't forget to pick up a garlic braid, necklace, or headband. Then head to Gourmet Alley and chow down on some of the festival's famous calamari or on their pepper steak sandwiches. Be prepared—about a quarter of a million people flock to Gilroy for the festival, so get there early and be patient. For more information, contact the Gilroy Garlic Festival at (408) 842-1635.

■ ROASTED GARLIC AND LEEK CHOWDER ■

This is one of my favorites. The garlic can also be roasted, unpeeled, in a 350° F oven for 25 minutes, then peeled and mashed.

1 tablespoon unsalted butter
6 large garlic cloves
1/3 cup diced salt pork (1 ounce)
3 medium leeks, whites and tender greens, chopped
2 medium carrots, diced
1 celery rib with leaves, finely chopped
4 cups chicken stock or broth

2 cups water
2 medium baked potatoes (about 1 pound), peeled and cut into 1/2-inch cubes
1 teaspoon chopped fresh sage
Salt and freshly ground pepper
1 tablespoon chopped fresh parsley

1. Melt the butter in a small skillet over low heat. Add the garlic cloves; cover and cook, turning once, until tender, about 25 minutes. The garlic will become golden, but be very careful not to let it burn. When soft, mash the garlic to form a smooth paste.

2. Meanwhile, cook the salt pork in boiling water for 3 minutes. Drain and pat dry.

3. Fry the salt pork in a medium saucepan over medium-low heat until golden. Discard all but 1 tablespoon of grease and add the leeks. Cook, stirring constantly, for 1 minute. Stir in the garlic paste and cook for 1 minute. Stir in the carrots and celery. Reduce the heat to medium-low and cook, covered, stirring occasionally, until the vegetables have softened, about 10 minutes.

4. Add the chicken stock and water to the vegetable mixture. Heat to boiling and add the potatoes. Return to boiling, reduce the heat, and simmer until the potatoes are tender, about 15 minutes.

5. Transfer 1 cup of the chowder (using mostly potatoes) to a food processor or blender. Process until smooth; be careful, as hot liquid will expand. Return the puree to the pot and stir in the sage. Add salt and pepper to taste and sprinkle with parsley.

SERVES 4

■ AUGUST ■

The Flowers withered on their stems,
The leaves hung limp and wan,
Within the trees a wistful breeze
Whispered and was gone;
The sky reached down a searing hand
And pressed upon the wearied land.

—ANNE MARY LAWLER

August was named after Augustus Caesar, Julius's adopted son and heir, in 8 B.C., but it was originally named *Sextilis,* as it was the sixth month in the Roman ten-month calendar. The Anglo-Saxon name was *Weod-monath,* or the "month in which weeds flourish." (It is thought that "weeds" referred to all vegetation.)

❋

■ AUGUST—SPECIAL EVENTS ■

NATIONAL CATFISH MONTH: Sponsored by the Mississippi catfish industry to encourage consumption of farm-raised Mississippi catfish.

IF YOU LIKE BEANS, Tracy, California, is the place to be during the first weekend in August. The folks in Tracy, the center of California's bean-growing region, take their beans seriously. They have even opened a bean museum, which is not as silly as it might sound, when you consider that the bean (along with corn and squash) is one of the "big three" native American food plants. In any case, the museum houses an impressive display of bean harvesters, both old and new. While you're there, delve into the history of the remarkable bean and learn all you want to know about its agricultural development and nutritional value—which is enormous. The highlight of the festival is a walk down "Bean Boulevard," where you can sample such dishes as bean salad, bean soup, chili, creole beans, Portuguese beans, tostadas, tamales, and tacos. For more information, contact the Tracy Chamber of Commerce at (209) 835-2131.

CALIFORNIA
DRY · BEAN
FESTIVAL
TRACY

■ WHITE BEAN SOUP ■

I usually use great Northern beans for this soup, though navy beans or other small white beans are also good.

1 pound dried white beans
¼ cup olive oil
1 medium Spanish onion, chopped
4 cloves garlic, minced
2 ribs celery, chopped
1 small red bell pepper, seeded and chopped
1 large green bell pepper, seeded and chopped

1 jalapeño pepper, seeded and deveined
1½ to 2 pounds smoked ham hocks, excess fat removed
6 cups chicken stock or broth
2 cups water
1 bay leaf
Salt and freshly ground pepper
½ cup chopped fresh parsley

1. Soak the beans overnight in cold water to cover. (Or place them in a large saucepan, cover with cold water, heat to boiling, and boil for 2 minutes. Remove from the heat and let stand, covered, for 1 hour.) Drain.

2. Heat the oil in a large heavy pot or Dutch oven over medium-low heat. Add the onion; cook for 1 minute. Add the garlic, celery, red and green bell peppers, and the jalapeño pepper. Cook, stirring constantly, for 1 minute. Add the ham hocks, chicken stock, water, and bay leaf. Heat to boiling, reduce the heat to medium-low, and simmer, covered, stirring occasionally, until the beans are tender, about 1½ hours. Remove from the heat and cool slightly.

3. Discard the bay leaf. Remove the ham hocks and cut off the meat. Chop into pieces and set aside.

4. Puree 4 cups of the mixture (mostly beans) in two batches in a food processor. Return the puree to the soup. Add the ham pieces and reheat until warmed through. Add salt and pepper to taste. Stir in the parsley just before serving.

SERVES 6 TO 8

✳

WINTER HARBOR LOBSTER FESTIVAL— SECOND SATURDAY IN AUGUST

WINTER HARBOR, MAINE, plays host to this annual festival, which celebrates one of Maine's most famous products—the lobster. In my opinion, the fame is well deserved. Perhaps it's the icy waters off the coast that make Maine lobsters the world's best. I don't know, I just know that they are, and, in my book, it's worth a trip to Maine anytime just to eat lobster at its freshest and best. A whole festival devoted to lobster is just too much to resist. Most of the festival events take place in Winter Harbor, where extra parking is provided. The "lobster feed" itself, however, takes place out at Frazer Point, about four miles away in Acadia National Park. Shuttle-bus service is provided. The lobsters at the festival are steamed on the beach, as in a clambake, and served with corn and a muffin. Lobster at its best! For more information, contact the Winter Harbor Chamber of Commerce at (207) 963-5561.

■ LOBSTER—BOILED, STEAMED, OR BROILED ■

Everyone, it seems, has a preference when it comes to how his or her lobster is prepared. Nothing beats a steamed, right-out-of-the-water lobster served on a rocky Maine beach, but if you aren't lucky enough to be in Maine, the three standard ways to prepare lobster follow. And no matter how it's fixed, don't forget the lemon wedges and drawn butter.

1 live lobster per person   Lemon wedges
Unsalted butter, melted

1. *To boil:* Heat a large pot of seawater or well-salted water to a boil. Plunge the lobsters into the pot head first. Cover the pot loosely and, when the water returns to a boil, boil the lobsters until done, about 10 minutes for a $1\frac{1}{4}$- to $1\frac{1}{2}$-pound lobster. Remove with tongs, allowing the lobsters to drain over the pot. Split the shells, crack the claws, and serve hot with butter and lemon wedges.

2. *To steam:* Place 1 inch of salted (or sea) water in a steamer or lobster pot. Place the lobsters in the top section of the pot. Cover and steam over boiling water until done, about 15 minutes. Remove and serve as above.

3. *To broil:* Place the lobsters, shell sides up, on a board and plunge a large sharp knife into the segment where the tail meets the body. This severs the spinal cord, instantly killing the lobster (though muscle reflexes will last longer). Crack the claws, then turn the lobsters over and split them in half lengthwise without cutting all the way through. Remove the sac from behind the head and lungs. Leave any coral (roe) intact. Brush the surface with melted butter and broil about 4 inches from the heat until done, 10 to 12 minutes. Serve with butter and lemon wedges.

✳

INTER-TRIBAL INDIAN CEREMONIAL—
SECOND WEEKEND IN AUGUST

IN GALLUP, New Mexico, this is said to be the oldest and largest exposition of Native American Pueblo and Plains cultures. The Pueblo Indians include the Zuni, Hopi, Taos, Acoma, San Idelfonso, and Zia. The Plains Indians include the Navajos, Kiowas, and Apaches, among others. The powwow actually begins on Wednesday and features a Plains dancing competition, an arts show, and a Western-style barbecue. To participate in the Saturday parade, one must be a Native American. Only the best of Native American artists and craftspeople are featured, and serious collectors flock to this show annually. The food is Native American, as well: corn stew with mutton, red and green chiles, oven bread, fry bread, and Indian tacos (fry bread, page 116) covered with a layer of fried hamburger, followed by shredded lettuce, cheddar cheese, chopped onion, diced tomato, and red or green chile). For more information, contact the Inter-Tribal Indian Ceremonial at (800) 233-4528.

■ GREEN TOMATO STEW ■

The following recipe is freely adapted from the Southwest Indian Cookbook, *a charming little book by Marcia Keegan. It is a great way to use green tomatoes—and much better for you than frying them.*

1/2 cup all-purpose flour
Salt and freshly ground pepper
2 pounds boneless beef chuck, cut into
    1-inch cubes
3 or 4 tablespoons vegetable oil (or lard
    or bacon drippings)
1 large onion, chopped
1 large clove garlic, minced
1 small hot green pepper, seeded and
    minced

2 cups beef stock or broth
    (approximately)
4 medium-size green tomatoes (about 2
    pounds), sliced
1 can (4 ounces) mild green chiles,
    drained and chopped
2 cups fresh corn kernels (from 4 large
    ears)
Chopped fresh parsley

1. Preheat the oven to 350° F.

2. Combine the flour with 1 teaspoon salt and 1/2 teaspoon ground pepper on a plate. Coat the beef pieces with the flour mixture. Set aside excess flour.

3. Heat 2 tablespoons of oil in a medium-large pot until hot. Brown the pieces of beef, about a quarter at a time, adding more oil as needed and transferring to a plate when browned.

4. If there is excess fat in the pot, discard all but 1 tablespoon. Add the onion; cook over medium-low heat for 2 minutes. Add the garlic and hot green pepper; cook for 4 minutes. Return the meat and sprinkle with 2 tablespoons of the reserved flour mixture. Cook, stirring constantly, for 2 minutes. Slowly stir in 1 cup of stock, scraping the bottom and sides of pot with a heavy wooden spoon. Add the tomatoes, mild chiles, and remaining 1 cup stock. Heat to boiling; cover, and bake in the oven for 1 hour, stirring occasionally.

5. Stir the corn into the stew and continue to bake, stirring occasionally and adding more stock if the stew becomes too thick, until the meat is tender, about 1 hour longer. Add salt and pepper to taste. Sprinkle with parsley and serve with rice.

SERVES 4

✳

HOPE WATERMELON FESTIVAL—
THIRD WEEK IN AUGUST

EVERY AUGUST, Hope, Arkansas (where President Clinton was born), plays host to more than 40,000 people at its annual watermelon harvest festival. Hope claims the world's largest melon ever, weighing in at around 200 pounds. Yearly, 100-pounders lie around attracting no special attention whatsoever, as they're so common. This is an old-fashioned kind of fair, with watermelon upon watermelon, of course, a fish fry complete with homemade ice cream, arts-and-crafts exhibits, country music, log rolling, wrestling, barrel racing, and the like. And now that Clinton has put Hope on the map, it is sure to attract even more people. For more information, contact the Hope-Hempstead County Chamber of Commerce at (501) 777-3640.

▪ FRIED WATERMELON RINDS ▪

Nathalie Dupree, television personality and cookbook author, is a good friend. Her recipe for watermelon rinds comes from one of her first major hits, New Southern Cooking *(Knopf, 1986). Nathalie's method for preparing the rinds is as follows: Peel the rinds with a knife by cutting off the dark green outside skin and inner layer down to the white part. Then cut the white part into ¹/₂-inch cubes.*

²/₃ cup cornmeal	Freshly ground black pepper
²/₃ cup all-purpose flour	1 cup shortening or vegetable oil
2 teaspoons salt	4 cups cubed peeled watermelon rind

1. Combine the cornmeal, flour, salt, and pepper to taste on a plate.
2. Heat the oil in a large heavy skillet until hot but not smoking.
3. Roll the rind in the cornmeal mixture. Gently place in the hot oil and fry until

lightly browned, about 8 to 10 minutes. Stir gently and continue to cook until browned all over, 4 to 5 minutes longer. Drain on paper towels. Sprinkle with more salt and pepper. Serve hot.

MAKES 4 CUPS

❋

HAYWARD ZUCCHINI FESTIVAL — THIRD WEEKEND IN AUGUST

THERE IS A BIT of farmer's wisdom that says that vegetables should be gathered only in the cool of the morning or as dusk settles in for the night—never, never in the heat of the day, especially if the sun is shining down brightly. If you choose to ignore this bit of advice, beware: your vegetables will discolor and become tough. Zucchini is a good example, and the folks in Hayward, California, do get up awfully early to pick the zucchini for their annual zucchini festival. You'll find every kind of zucchini dish you could imagine here: zucchini bread and cake, zucchini tempura, zucchini nachos, fries, and chips, and many more dishes that you may not have thought of before. There is a growing contest (size) and a carving contest (shape). Entertainment includes rock and roll, belly dancers, comedians, gospel music, and a Broadway serenade. For more information, contact the Hayward Zucchini Festival at (510) 581-4364.

▪ ZUCCHINI MUFFIN GEMS ▪

*T*his is probably the best recipe on earth for zucchini muffins. They are truly superb. The recipe itself is a legacy of the Toblin family, of San Diego, and was passed on by a mutual friend, Jody Gillis.

½ cup sugar
1 large egg, lightly beaten
¼ cup vegetable oil
¾ cup all-purpose flour
¼ teaspoon baking powder
¼ teaspoon baking soda

¼ teaspoon salt
¼ teaspoon freshly grated nutmeg
1 cup grated zucchini (about ¼ pound)
¼ cup raisins, finely chopped
¼ cup chopped pecans

1. Preheat the oven to 350° F. In a large bowl, combine the sugar, egg, and oil. Mix well.

2. In a medium bowl, sift the flour with the baking powder, baking soda, salt, and nutmeg. Stir this into the sugar-egg mixture.

3. Add the zucchini, raisins, and pecans, and stir only until mixed; do not overwork. Spoon the batter into a well-buttered 9-cup muffin tin, filling each cup about two-thirds full. Bake until the muffins are golden brown and a toothpick inserted in the center comes out clean, about 25 minutes. Run a knife around the edges to loosen.

MAKES 9 MUFFINS

❋

STATE OF MAINE BLUEBERRY FESTIVAL — LAST FULL WEEK IN AUGUST

SOME 10,000 PEOPLE show up in Union, Maine, for the annual blueberry festival, which is proffered in conjunction with the Union County Fair. Each day begins with a pancake breakfast, served by the "Blueberry Queen" herself (with some help from her attending "princesses"). Later on, there's a pie-baking competition and a pie-eating contest. You can buy baskets of fresh blueberries, as well as home-made blueberry jam, candy, ice cream, and juice, and sample home-cooked blueberry dishes made by local vendors. For collectors, souvenir T-shirts, hats, bags, and postcards feature the blueberry. The Union County Fair is a full-scale country fair with horse and oxen pulls, pig chasing, 4-H exhibits, and so forth. For more information, contact the Union Fair at (207) 785-4180.

▪ BLUEBERRY MUFFINS ▪

*T*he *blueberry muffin is probably the most popular muffin in the entire country. There are hundreds of recipes for this classic use of the blueberry. Mine is flavored with grated orange peel.*

1 cup blueberries, picked over
2 cups all-purpose flour
½ cup sugar
1 tablespoon baking powder
½ teaspoon salt

1 egg, lightly beaten
1 teaspoon finely grated orange peel
¼ cup unsalted butter, melted
1 cup milk (or half milk and half buttermilk)

1. Preheat the oven to 375° F. Grease the cups of a 12-muffin pan.
2. Toss the blueberries with ¼ cup flour in a bowl. Set aside.
3. Sift the remaining flour with the sugar, baking powder, and salt into a large bowl. Stir in the egg, orange peel, butter, and milk. Fold in the blueberries.
4. Spoon the batter into the prepared pan, filling each cup about two-thirds full. Bake until golden and firm, 20 to 25 minutes. Cool in pan on a rack for 5 minutes before unmolding the muffins.

MAKES ABOUT 12 MUFFINS

FALL RECIPES

Cold Tenderloin of Pork with
Sweet Pepper Sauce

Green Chile Con Carne

Navajo Fry Bread

Grandmother Moehlenbrink's
Chocolate Cake

Crawfish Jambalaya

Calf Fry

Amy's Fried Frogs' Legs

Cape Cod Cranberry Bread Pudding

Traditional Honey Cake

Cinnamon Ice Cream

Old-Fashioned Apple Pie

Roast Goose

Ham with Redeye Gravy

Pan-Fried Trout

Grilled Alligator Tail

Fettuccine with Walnuts and Avocado

The Best-Ever Crab Dip

Apple Strudel

Norwegian Beef Stew

Oysters on the Half Shell

Anna Teresa Callen's Incredible Lasagna

Reuben Sandwich

Black-Walnut Brownies

Marinated Brussels Sprouts

Pumpkin Cookies

Garlicky Braised Eggplant

North Carolina Moppin' Sauce

Ghoulish Gruel

The Best Pecan Pie

Turkey Club Sandwich

Tropical Grilled Flank Steak with
Fresh-Fruit Salsa

Hungarian Chicken

The Ancient New England Standing
Dish of Pompion

Melon Jam

Iced Scones

FALL

❁

FALL IS my favorite season. Farm stands are bursting at the seams with an abundance of fruits and vegetables. Fresh, crisp apples from local orchards make the best, juiciest pies of the year. The pumpkins that so gloriously dot the landscape lie ripe for the picking. The cauliflower is dazzlingly white, and the Brussels sprouts cling to their center stems, just waiting to be plucked and cooked. It truly is a magical season.

As a youngster in Colorado, I loved the splendor of golden-yellow aspen leaves shimmering amidst stately evergreens. A drive in the mountains with my siblings became a ritual, with my older brother, Mark, inevitably at the wheel. More often than not, our foray took us high into snow country, where we just couldn't resist stopping to toss a few snowballs, even if dressed in shorts more suitable to lower (and warmer) altitudes. One of the images that sticks with me most, however, is one autumnal stroll through the cemetery that sits high above Central City. Headstones dating back to the 1800s told the sad tales of many very short lives—husbands, wives, and babies who never lived to see their first birthdays—a testament to the pain and struggle of those pioneer days. More than anything else, I now think, I was struck by the overwhelming sense of history emanating from the spot. Perhaps it was inevitable that I would be drawn to the Northeast, where grave markers date back to the 1600s; where the pervasive, almost ghostly, aura of colonial America hangs like a whisper over the entire region; and where the New England countryside comes ablaze with fall colors so brilliant they sometimes take your breath away.

My fall sojourns these days usually take me to Vermont, where my heart, if not as yet, my physical being, resides. Aside from the glorious foliage, nothing in life is sweeter than a trek in the woods that yields the discovery of a long-abandoned apple orchard, the trees still bearing their fruit: crisp sweet apples, somewhat worm-worn and bird-pecked, but tinged with pink straight through to the core—the best I have ever eaten.

In the late fall, the smell of wood smoke permeates Vermont's West River Valley, beckoning to the senses. Wood fires have always given me great comfort, but I have never looked at them quite the way Thomas Bailey Aldrich (1836–1907) did in *Miss Mehitable's Son:*

What is more cheerful, now, in the fall of the year, than an open-wood-fire? Do you hear those little chirps and twitters coming out of that piece of apple-wood? Those are the ghosts of the robins and blue-birds that sang upon the bough when it was in blossom last Spring. In Summer whole flocks of them come fluttering about the fruit-trees under the window: so I have singing birds all the year round.

Fall, of course, is the time for harvesting—and for giving thanks. It is a season that most colorfully takes us from the greens of summer to the grays of winter, with the promise of a white Christmas right around the corner.

❊

■ SEPTEMBER ■

The morrow was a bright September morn;
The earth was beautiful as if new-born;
There was that nameless splendor everywhere
That wild exhilaration in the air . . .

—HENRY WADSWORTH LONGFELLOW

September was the seventh month in the old Roman calendar. When it became the ninth month of the Julian calendar, its name remained the same. Although Julius Caesar gave the month thirty-one days, Augustus later stole one and added it to August (then *Sextilis*). It is the month of the harvest moon—the moon that rises over the horizon at sunset, giving farmers extra light in which to gather their crops. This phenomenon occurs on those days of the first full moon nearest the autumnal equinox. September is often called the "harvest month" and is brimming with festivals and fairs, agricultural and otherwise.

❋

■ SEPTEMBER SPECIAL EVENTS ■

ALL-AMERICAN BREAKFAST MONTH: Sponsored by the National Livestock and Meat Board to promote the use of pork, beef, and lamb for breakfast.

NATIONAL CHICKEN MONTH: Sponsored by the National Broiler Council to celebrate the nutritious, economic, convenient, and versatile aspects of the chicken—and, most importantly, to teach people how to handle and prepare the birds safely.

NATIONAL RICE MONTH: Sponsored by the USA Rice Council, as a salute to the U.S. rice industry.

✳

LABOR DAY—
FIRST MONDAY IN SEPTEMBER

IN 1882, Peter J. Maguire, a labor union leader, came up with the notion that one day a year should be set aside in honor of the working person. He pointed out that other holidays commemorated religious, civil, and military events, but none celebrated the country's "backbone"—the working force of the nation. He suggested the first Monday in September, as it was conveniently situated "nearly midway between the Fourth of July and Thanksgiving, and would fill a gap in the chronology of legal holidays." The first Labor Day, in that same year, drew 10,000 workers to Union Square in New York City, where they celebrated with a parade, speeches, and a picnic. Labor Day became, in effect, the unofficial opening of the fall political season, marking the beginning of intense campaigning as candidates focused their attention on the November elections. (The day's "legal holiday" status came in 1894, when it was officially sanctioned by Congress and signed into law by President Grover Cleveland.)

Labor Day weekend now serves as much as a send-off to summer as a herald of fall. Summer is over. It's time to get the kids ready for school and gear up for the coming harvest. There is a change in the air—it's a nice day for a picnic. So, whether you throw your blanket on the beach or on a mountaintop, or just set a table in the backyard as I do, follow my advice: Keep it simple—and festive. It is, after all, the beginning of a new season.

★ ★ ★

COLD TENDERLOIN OF PORK
WITH SWEET PEPPER SAUCE

One of my favorite picnic foods is tenderloin of pork that has been marinated in a smoky, red-pepper marinade, then roasted and cooled. The tenderloin, for some reason, is a remarkably underutilized cut of pork. As the name implies, it is extremely tender, and it cooks very quickly. The meat should be sliced before leaving home and kept reasonably cool until it is served. Pass the extra sauce on the side. Add some garden-fresh salad, some crusty bread, a glass of wine—and you're in business. This pork is also great hot and can easily be prepared on the grill. (To grill, sear the meat over medium-hot coals for 2 minutes per side. Then, grill, covered, turning once, about 25 minutes.)

1 large red bell pepper
1 clove garlic
1/3 cup heavy cream
6 tablespoons (3/4 stick) unsalted butter
2 tablespoons tomato paste
1 teaspoon chopped fresh sage,
    or 1 teaspoon crumbled dried sage

1 teaspoon Hungarian sweet paprika
1/2 teaspoon salt
4 small pork tenderloins (1/2 to 3/4 pound
    each)

1. Roast the pepper directly over a gas flame or under a broiler, as close to the heat as possible, turning, until charred all over. Wrap the pepper in paper towels and place in a plastic bag. Let stand until cool. Rub off the skin with paper towels. Core the pepper and coarsely chop.

2. Place the chopped pepper and the garlic in a food processor or blender. With the machine on, slowly add the cream and process just until smooth, about 30 seconds.

3. In a medium saucepan, melt the butter over moderately low heat. Whisk in the tomato paste, pepper-garlic puree, sage, paprika, and salt. Heat through for about 1 minute, but do not boil. Set the pepper sauce aside and let cool.

4. Brush the tenderloins with about one-fourth of the sauce and let stand, covered, at room temperature for 2 hours, or refrigerate overnight.

5. Preheat the oven to 350° F and reheat the remaining sauce until warm. Bake the tenderloins on a rack, basting with the sauce every 10 minutes, until the internal temperature reaches 160° F on a meat thermometer—about 50 minutes.

SERVES 8

❋

HATCH CHILE FESTIVAL—
LABOR DAY WEEKEND

SOME SAY that the world's best chiles grow in New Mexico, and for chile lovers, this festival at the Hatch airport is the ultimate gustatory delight. It's not a fancy affair—the peppers are the lone attraction—but there sure are peppers here: tons of them, from mild to incredibly incendiary. Fresh or dried, green, red, or yellow— this is where you find them. You will also find a large variety of traditional Mexican-American fare to nibble on. One of the festival's culinary attractions is a green chile con carne that has been lovingly prepared, pampered over a low flame for five full days. There are other "chile'd" goods to sample, as well: chile bread, chile salsa, chile jelly, and even a chile wine. For more information, contact the Hatch Valley Chamber of Commerce at (505) 267-5050.

▪ GREEN CHILE CON CARNE ▪

If you don't live in the western part of the United States, chances are you aren't going to find "long greens," or New Mexican chiles outside a can. This recipe uses roasted bell peppers for texture and canned peppers for taste. When I can find poblano peppers, I use them as well.

4 large green bell peppers
4 tablespoons lard or vegetable
   shortening
2 pounds boneless chuck steak,
   chopped into ⅛-inch cubes
1 large onion, chopped
1 large clove garlic, minced

2 jalapeño peppers (or more, to taste),
   seeded, deveined, and minced
¼ cup all-purpose flour
2 cups beef broth
4 cans (4 ounces each) green chiles
Salt and freshly ground pepper

1. Roast the bell peppers over a gas flame or under a broiler until charred all over. Carefully wrap them in paper towels and place them in a plastic bag. Let stand for 5 minutes, then rub the skins from the peppers with paper towels. Core and chop the peppers. Reserve.

2. In a large heavy pot, heat the lard or oil over medium-high heat until hot but not smoking. Add a quarter of the meat and sauté until lightly browned. Transfer to a bowl with a slotted spoon. Continue to sauté the meat in batches until all of it is browned.

3. Return the meat to the pot and add the onion. Cook, stirring constantly, until lightly browned, about 4 minutes. Add the garlic and jalapeño pepper and reduce the heat to low.

4. Sprinkle the flour over the meat mixture. Cook, stirring constantly, for 2 minutes. Stir in the beef broth and reserved chopped pepper. Cook, covered, stirring occasionally, until the meat is tender, about 1 hour and 15 minutes.

5. Drain and chop the canned peppers. Add to the chile mixture. Continue to cook, covered, for 30 minutes. Add salt and pepper to taste. (Remove the cover and raise the heat slightly if the chile is too thin.)

SERVES 4 TO 6

THIS THREE-DAY EVENT held in Santa Fe, New Mexico, celebrates the peaceful resettlement of *Nuevo Mexico* by the Spanish colonists. Santa Fe was first settled by the Spanish around 1609. They lived fairly peacefully with the native inhabitants until 1680, when the Indians revolted and just about wiped out the Spanish population. In 1692 General Don Diego de Vargas was sent in to reclaim the settlement for Spain. It is said that he prayed to Mother Mary and promised that if God helped him resettle the town without bloodshed, he would hold a fiesta every year in gratitude. Mother Mary and God listened, and the religious roots of the festival are still evident. Each day begins with a special mass. There is the General Don Diego de Vargas Mass, the Mariachi Mass, and the Mass of Thanksgiving. Other highlights include the *Baile de Gente* ("Dance of the People") with its burning of *Zozobra* (Old Man Gloom), the *Entrada* (reenactment of the resettlement), the Procession of the Cross of the Martyrs, the *Gran Carreada* (Mexican rodeo), Navajo dances, and music, arts, and crafts. The foods featured are Navajo and Mexican-American. For more information, contact the Santa Fe Fiesta Council at (505) 988-7575.

▪ NAVAJO FRY BREAD ▪

Indian "fry bread" is very popular at fairs and festivals that celebrate Native American culture. What makes this bread "Navajo" is the hole in the middle—the Navajos traditionally lowered their dough into hot fat with a stick inserted through the center.

2 cups all-purpose flour	½ cup warm water
2 teaspoons baking powder	Vegetable oil for frying
1 teaspoon salt	

1. In a large bowl, combine the flour, baking powder, and salt. Slowly add the water, working it into the flour with your fingers until a dough is formed. Knead briefly on a floured board. Cover and let stand for 1 hour.

2. Knead the dough briefly a second time and let stand, covered, for 10 minutes.

3. Heat about 1 inch of oil in a 10-inch skillet until hot but not smoking.

4. Tear off 1½-inch pieces of dough. Roll each piece out on a floured board into a circle about ¼ inch thick. Poke a hole in the center with a fork. Fry for about 2 minutes per side. Drain on paper towels.

MAKES ABOUT 10 PIECES

THIS DAY was established in honor not only of grandparents but of all older men and women whose wisdom and strengths we would be wise to share. In the kitchen, as well. With our modern kitchens and ubiquitous microwaves, our youngsters are growing up in a generation that will look back on frozen dinners as comfort food. Family recipes get lost to memory on the way. And with them goes part of the family history. So if *your* grandmother has never written down her family recipes, help her to do so—you will always be happy that you did. My grandparents are long dead, but my Grandmother Moehlenbrink's chocolate cake lives on forever. Food is history. To trace the distribution of the world's food supply and how it was prepared is to trace mankind itself.

■ GRANDMOTHER MOEHLENBRINK'S ■ CHOCOLATE CAKE

My Grandmother Moehlenbrink always called this her "goodie cake." As kids we called it "soap cake"—why, I'll never know. Grandma never frosted hers, but I sometimes sprinkle mine with confectioners' sugar.

2 large eggs
Pinch salt
1 cup mild-tasting vegetable oil
1 cup buttermilk
2 cups sugar
1/4 cup unsweetened cocoa (preferably
　Lindt or Droste's)

3 cups sifted all-purpose flour
1 tablespoon baking soda
1 cup very hot water
Confectioners' sugar

1. Preheat the oven to 325° F. Grease and flour a 9 x 13-inch glass cake pan. If using a pan not made of glass, preheat the oven to 350° F.

2. In the large bowl of an electric mixer, beat the eggs with the salt until light. Slowly add the oil and buttermilk. Beat well. Beat in the sugar.

3. On low speed, slowly add the cocoa, flour, baking soda, and water to the buttermilk mixture. Beat only until mixed. Pour the mixture into the prepared pan. Bake until a toothpick inserted in the center comes out clean, about 50 minutes. Cool on a wire rack. Sprinkle with confectioners' sugar before serving.

SERVES ABOUT 10

✳

FESTIVALS ACADIENS —
THIRD WEEKEND IN SEPTEMBER

HELD IN Lafayette, Louisiana, in the heart of Cajun country, this is actually several festivals tied together to celebrate the culture of the French Acadians who were brutally exiled from Nova Scotia by the British around 1785. Highlights include historical presentations, demonstrations of Cajun arts and crafts, and a film festival, but the most important event, for food lovers anyway, is the Bayou Food Festival. There you can succumb to crawfish pies, jambalayas, gumbos, *étouffées, andouille* and *boudin* (sausages), rice and beans, and other regional delights—so bring your appetite. For more information, contact the Lafayette Convention and Visitors Commission at (318) 232-3808.

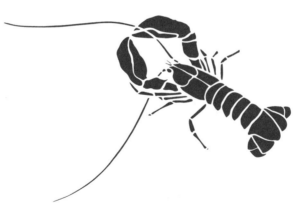

▪ CRAWFISH JAMBALAYA ▪

Chowing down on a platter of plain boiled crawfish is one of the great advantages of living in Cajun country. One learns very quickly how to snap off the head, suck out the rich fat (called the "butter"), and pick out the tail meat. Most gourmet stores in the U.S. sell frozen crawfish tails with accumulated fat. Medium cleaned shrimp can be substituted.

¼ cup vegetable or olive oil
1 cup diced cooked ham (about ½ pound)
1 large onion, finely chopped
3 cloves garlic, minced
½ cup chopped celery
1 small green bell pepper, seeded and chopped
1 pound peeled fresh or frozen (thawed) crawfish tails with accumulated fat

1½ cups clam juice
1½ cups chicken broth (approximately)
1 large tomato, chopped
¼ cup chopped scallions, white and green parts
½ teaspoon cayenne
½ teaspoon salt
¼ teaspoon freshly ground black pepper
1 cup uncooked long-grain rice
¼ cup chopped fresh parsley

1. Heat the oil in a medium-size heavy pot until hot but not smoking. Sauté the ham, stirring occasionally, until lightly browned. Add the onion; cook for 1 minute. Add the garlic; cook for 4 minutes.

2. Add the celery, green pepper, and crawfish to the ham mixture. Stir in the clam juice and chicken broth, scraping the bottom and sides of the pot. Add the tomato, scallions, cayenne, salt, and black pepper. Heat to boiling. Stir in the rice and return to boiling. Reduce the heat and cook, covered, over medium-low heat, adding more chicken broth if needed, until the rice is tender, about 25 minutes.

SERVES 4 TO 6

❉

THE ADVENTUROUS won't want to miss this festival, which is held in Vinita, Oklahoma. For the kids, there are egg tosses, turtle races, bubble-gum-blowing contests, and plain-old "moseying." For the brave, there are "hairiest legs" and "liars" contests and the "calf-fry" cook-off and lunch. ("Calf fry," incidentally, is another name for Rocky Mountain or prairie oysters—i.e., testicles.) For more information, contact the Vinita Chamber of Commerce at (918) 256-7133.

▪ CALF FRY ▪

Calves' testicles are available from time to time at specialty butchers—and at roundup time on the ranch. The following recipe is just a guide. Feel free to be inventive.

Calves' testicles	Salt and freshly ground pepper
Salted water	Bacon drippings
Fine cracker crumbs	

1. Soak the testicles in salted water (1 teaspoon salt for each quart of water) for 1 hour. Drain.

2. Season the cracker crumbs with salt and pepper. Place them on a plate and roll the testicles in the crumbs.

3. Heat enough bacon drippings to film an 8-inch skillet until hot, but not smoking. Sauté the testicles until well browned and warmed through.

❋

RAYNE, LOUISIANA, is the self-proclaimed "Frog Capital of the World," and what better place to have a festival? The festivities kick off with a *fais dodo,* the Cajun equivalent of a hoe-down, where the gumbo, beer, and music seem to be in limitless supply. This festival is about twenty years old and going strong. There are frog-jumping contests, frog-eating contests, a Mr. and Ms. Tadpole contest, cooking contests, lots of frogs' legs to snack on, and some of the best Cajun music on tap anywhere. The Acadian city of Rayne "gar-on-tees" that you will "pass a good time." For more information, contact the Rayne Chamber of Commerce and Agriculture at (318) 334-2332.

▪ AMY'S FRIED FROGS' LEGS ▪

This recipe won one of the honorable mentions garnered in 1991 by then—eighth grader Amy Pastor.

6 to 8 frogs' legs (cleaned)
1 can (12 ounces) evaporated milk
2 eggs
1 tablespoon baking powder
2 tablespoons vinegar

Oil for deep frying
Salt and freshly ground black pepper
Cayenne
1 cup all-purpose flour

1. Place the frogs' legs in a glass or ceramic dish.

2. In a mixing bowl, combine the evaporated milk, eggs, baking powder, and vinegar. Whisk well and pour over the frogs' legs. Cover and marinate for at least 1 hour.

3. In a large heavy pot or saucepan, heat enough oil to reach at least halfway up the sides of the frogs' legs. The temperature should be about 380° F.

4. Meanwhile, drain the frogs' legs and lightly pat them dry with paper towels. Sprinkle with salt, black pepper, and cayenne to taste. Roll in flour and fry in hot oil until golden brown, about 10 minutes.

SERVES 3 OR 4

✳

CRANBERRY HARVEST FESTIVAL—SECOND FRIDAY
THROUGH THIRD SUNDAY IN SEPTEMBER

TO CELEBRATE the cranberry harvest, the folks in Harwich, Massachusetts, on Cape Cod throw a yearly festival that begins on the second Friday of September with the Cranberry Ball. Over the next nine days, you can visit flooded bogs to see how cranberries are harvested, and enjoy jamborees, fireworks, contests, and a big parade on the final Sunday. Needless to say, there are cranberry treats of all kinds to be sampled and/or carried home. For more information, contact the Harwich Chamber of Commerce at (508) 432-1600.

▪ CAPE COD CRANBERRY BREAD PUDDING ▪

This is one of my all-time favorite recipes. Homemade cranberry sauce is a necessity, however. You might wish to double the portion for the cranberry sauce and save it, in a sterilized jar, for the holiday table.

1 large seedless orange	½ cup heavy cream
2 cups cranberries, picked over	3 tablespoons Grand Marnier liqueur
2¼ cups sugar	1 teaspoon vanilla extract
⅓ cup water	One 8-ounce loaf French- or Italian-
2 large eggs	style bread, trimmed of crust and cut
Pinch of ground cinnamon	into thin slices
1½ cups milk	Heavy cream

1. Finely grate the peel from the orange. Remove the skin and membranes from the orange. Section the orange and cut each section across into thin slices. Combine the orange peel, the orange slices, the cranberries, 1½ cups sugar, and the water in a medium saucepan. Heat to boiling; reduce the heat. Simmer covered 10 minutes. Remove cover and continue to cook until slightly thickened, about 5 minutes. Remove from heat.

2. Preheat the oven to 325° F.

3. Beat the eggs with the cinnamon in a large bowl until light. Beat in the remaining ¾ cup sugar, the milk, the cream, the Grand Marnier, and the vanilla.

4. Place a layer of bread over the bottom of a buttered 2-quart soufflé dish. Using a ladle, add enough egg mixture to cover the bread. Spoon one third of the cranberry mixture over the top. Repeat the layers two more times adding all the egg mixture to the dish before spooning on the last third of the cranberries. Bake until firm, about 1 hour. Serve slightly warm or at room temperature with heavy cream.

SERVES 8

❊

JEWISH HIGH HOLY DAYS — GENERALLY IN SEPTEMBER

THE HIGH HOLY DAYS, referred to in Hebrew as *Yamim Noraim* (Days of Awe), begin with *Rosh Hashana,* the first two days of Tishri, the first month of the lunar new year. Owing to the peculiarities of the Hebrew calendar, Rosh Hashana can fall anytime between September 5 and October 5. The High Holy Days end ten days later, with *Yom Kippur,* the Day of Atonement, which is a fast day. It is a time for self-reflection and atonement, a time to make peace with one's enemies, and a time for optimism and hope for a "good and sweet" year ahead. Though customs vary, the holiday table reflects this hope. "Sweetness" is literally the rule. No sour or bitter foods are served. The new-year meal begins, just before sundown, with the mother of the household lighting the candles. A prayer (*kiddush*) is said, blessing the wine and a loaf of challah bread, decorated with birds or ladders so that the prayers may ascend to the heavens. A blessing is also said over slices of apples that have been dipped in honey, representing the hope for a sweet new year. The symbolic foods of Rosh Hashana include fish (fertility), challah bread (life without end), honey (sweetness), carrots (prosperity), and apples ("new" fruit).

■ TRADITIONAL HONEY CAKE ■

Honey cake, or leckach, *is a favorite dessert at this time of year. It is a wonderful confection, flavored with coffee, and it makes an appropriate house gift during the High Holy Days.*

1¾ cups dark honey
1 cup strong coffee
3½ cups sifted all-purpose flour
2 teaspoons baking powder
1 teaspoon baking soda
Pinch salt
1 teaspoon ground allspice

1 teaspoon ground cinnamon
¼ teaspoon ground cloves
¼ teaspoon ground nutmeg
4 eggs
2 tablespoons vegetable oil
1 cup sugar

1. Heat the honey slowly to boiling; remove from the heat and cool. Stir in the coffee.

2. Meanwhile, preheat the oven to 300° F. Grease and flour two 9 x 5-inch loaf pans.

3. Sift the flour with the baking powder, baking soda, salt, allspice, cinnamon, cloves, and nutmeg.

4. In a large bowl, lightly beat the eggs. Beat in the oil and sugar.

5. Add the dry ingredients to the wet ingredients in several batches, alternating with the coffee-honey mixture. Mix well and pour into the prepared pans. Bake until a toothpick inserted in the center comes out almost clean, about 1 hour. Cool the cakes in their pans on a rack. Loosen the cakes and leave them in the pans. Let stand, tightly covered, overnight to develop flavor.

MAKES 2 LOAF CAKES

DAY OF THE (ICE CREAM) CONE—SEPTEMBER 22

IT HAS OFTEN been said that the ice cream cone was born at the 1904 World's Fair in St. Louis when a Syrian immigrant named Hamwi offered a *zalabia* (Persian-style waffle) to an ice cream vendor for use as a "holder" when the latter's supply of dishes was depleted. Months before the fair, however, on September 22, 1903, an Italian immigrant, Italo Marchiony, filed an application for a patent for a cup mold with slanted sides. But Marchiony sold lemon ice, not ice cream, from a pushcart on the streets of New York, so perhaps both men deserve credit. In any case, for ice cream lovers, September 22 is the day to buy their favorite flavors. One scoop, or two?

▪ CINNAMON ICE CREAM ▪

I have yet to see a commercial ice cream flavored with cinnamon. It's surprising, considering that some of our best restaurant chefs are pairing cinnamon ice cream with pies and pastries in place of plain old vanilla. It's good, too. Try the following with your next apple or rhubarb pie.

¾ cup sugar (or to taste)
1 tablespoon ground cinnamon

2 cups light cream or half-and-half
2 cups heavy cream

1. In a medium saucepan, combine the sugar, cinnamon, and 1 cup light cream. Stir over medium heat just until the sugar has dissolved. Do not allow to boil. Remove from the heat and let stand, stirring occasionally, until cool.

2. Add the remaining light cream and the heavy cream to the mixture and pour into the canister of an ice cream freezer. Proceed according to the manufacturer's directions.

MAKES ABOUT 1 ½ QUARTS

AUTUMNAL EQUINOX—ON OR ABOUT SEPTEMBER 22

The autumnal equinox occurs about September 22, when the sun crosses the plane of the equator and night and day are of equal length all over the earth. From this point until the vernal equinox in the Northern Hemisphere, the nights will be longer than the days. The darkest day, and the end of fall, coincide with the arrival of the winter solstice (about December 22).

❉

JOHN CHAPMAN'S BIRTHDAY—
SEPTEMBER 26

IT SEEMS APPROPRIATE that apple harvest time falls around the birthday of John Chapman, known in American folklore as "Johnny Appleseed." Born in Massachusetts in 1774, he is often depicted as a wild-eyed, seed-scattering creature dressed in a gunny sack with a frying pan for a hat. This portrayal is frequently ridiculed, yet the public library of Fort Wayne, Indiana (where he died in 1845), has published a booklet that supports it. Though everyone agrees that he didn't run around throwing apple seeds here and there, there is some disagreement as to how he *did* plant his orchards. In his youth, Chapman was apprenticed to an orchardist in New England and learned much that he would use in later life. One legend holds that in his travels around the Midwest, he planted seedlings by the thousands and practiced the art of grafting. Another has it that he only planted seeds or young saplings that he acquired in Pennsylvania and never grafted anything, as he believed that the mere cutting of a branch caused pain to the tree. There is no question that he was a deeply religious man (he was a disciple of Emanuel Swedenborg) and was very close to nature. Whether or not he talked to the animals and walked barefoot among poisonous snakes, as some tales have it, doesn't really matter in the end. What does matter is that he played an important role in settling the Midwest, and many a pioneer was very grateful that Johnny Appleseed had gone before, leaving a bit of civilization—and an abundance of apples—in his wake.

Every year, on the third weekend in September, the Parks and Recreation Department of Fort Wayne hosts the Johnny Appleseed Festival, which attracts hundreds of thousands of visitors to his gravesite. All participants dress in 1800s attire to celebrate both the man and the pioneer spirit of the early frontier. There are myriad arts and crafts demonstrations, music, and storytelling hours. The local farmers bring in their produce to sell as well. For more information, contact the Fort Wayne Parks and Recreation Department at (219) 483-0057.

■ OLD-FASHIONED APPLE PIE ■

*A*pples were served in one form or another at almost every meal in eighteenth-century New England. In fact, New Englanders were often criticized for serving apple pie for breakfast. Frankly, I think they had the right idea.

PASTRY
2½ cups all-purpose flour
1 teaspoon sugar
½ teaspoon salt
½ cup (1 stick) unsalted butter, chilled
½ cup vegetable shortening, chilled
1 teaspoon finely grated orange peel
4 tablespoons orange juice

FILLING
3 pounds green apples (about 6 large)
⅓ cup plus 1½ tablespoons all-purpose flour

¾ cup granulated sugar
1 teaspoon ground cinnamon
⅛ teaspoon freshly grated nutmeg
1 teaspoon finely grated orange peel
1 teaspoon vanilla extract
½ cup honey
⅓ cup packed dark brown sugar
Pinch ground ginger
3½ tablespoons unsalted butter, chilled
1 large egg, beaten

1. *To make the pastry:* In a medium bowl, combine the flour with the sugar and salt. Cut in the butter, shortening, and orange peel with a knife. Blend with a pastry blender until the mixture has the texture of coarse crumbs. Add the orange juice, about a tablespoon at a time, and mix gently with a fork to form a soft dough. Do not overwork. Refrigerate for 1 hour.

2. *To make the filling:* Peel and core the apples, and slice them into a large bowl. Sprinkle with 1½ tablespoons flour, the granulated sugar, ½ teaspoon cinnamon, the nutmeg, orange peel, vanilla, and honey. Toss well. Let stand, tossing occasionally, for 30 minutes.

3. Preheat the oven to 450° F.

4. In a small bowl, combine the remaining ⅓ cup flour with the remaining ½ teaspoon cinnamon, the brown sugar, and the ginger. Mix well. Add 2 tablespoons

of butter and work the mixture with your fingers until it is mealy. Remove ¼ cup and set aside.

5. Roll out slightly more than half the pastry on a lightly floured board. Line a 9-inch pie plate with the pastry. Drain the apple slices, reserving the liquid. Layer the apples in the pastry shell, sprinkling with the flour mixture as you layer. Sprinkle the filling with 5 tablespoons of the reserved apple liquid. Dot the top with the remaining 1½ tablespoons butter.

6. Roll out the remaining pastry and cut it into ½-inch-wide strips. Weave the strips into a lattice pattern over the apples. Trim and flute the edges. Sprinkle the reserved ¼ cup flour mixture in the open spaces. Brush the pastry with beaten egg. Place the pie on a foil-lined baking sheet and bake for 15 minutes. Reduce the oven temperature to 350° F and bake, basting occasionally with any overflowing juices, until the crust is golden and the apples are tender, about 50 minutes longer.

SERVES 6 TO 8

MICHAELMAS is a religious feast day celebrating St. Michael and all guardian angels. St. Michael, the first archangel, was a warrior and a hero of battles. Churches and chapels all over Europe are dedicated to him. The most famous, perhaps, is the chapel and monastery that sits atop Mont Saint Michel, a mile off France's Brittany coast. Nobody is certain just how this feast day became associated with goose, but according to an old English proverb, "If you eat goose on Michaelmas Day, you will never want money all the year round." Even more mysterious is how the custom made its way to Mifflin County, Pennsylvania. Though often credited to the British, the tradition of "Goose Day" has also been linked to the Dutch. It has been suggested that it was brought to this country by the Amish, who emigrated to Pennsylvania via Holland. In any event, if you happen to be in the vicinity of Lewiston, Pennsylvania, on September 29, and you haven't been invited to someone's house for dinner, don't fret. Every restaurant in the county has goose on the menu. For more information, contact the Juniata Valley Area Chamber of Commerce at (717) 248-6714.

▪ ROAST GOOSE ▪

*T*he goose lovers of Mifflin County have the following advice for roasting your "good-luck" goose at home. (Note: A ten-pound bird will serve six.)

Prepare a young goose for roasting by removing the neck, giblets, and excess fat from the body cavity. Rinse the bird and drain.

Stuff with a mixture of apples, prunes, and raisins to flavor the goose and absorb excess fat. You will probably want to discard this stuffing at the end of the cooking time.

Roast, breast-side up, in a 400° F oven for about an hour (for a 10- to 12-pound bird), then reduce the temperature to 325° F for an additional 2 to 2½ hours. During roasting, spoon or siphon off accumulated fat at half-hour intervals. The goose is done when a meat thermometer inserted in the thigh registers 180–185° F.

❊

SOME FESTIVALS seem to make all the guidebooks, and this one, which takes place in Lebanon, Kentucky, about sixty miles southwest of Lexington, is one of them. Ham, like bourbon, is a specialty of Kentucky, and one of the features here is a breakfast of ham with redeye gravy, fried apples, sliced tomatoes, and, of course, biscuits. Food booths sell hams, ham biscuits, ham and beans, etc. While munching, you can take in the "pigasus" parade, the "pokey pig" run, pig-calling, and myriad other folk events. For more information, contact the Lebanon Chamber of Commerce at (512) 692-9594.

■ HAM WITH REDEYE GRAVY ■

This may not be the official version of this dish, but it just may be the best.

1 teaspoon unsalted butter
1 large ham steak (about ¹/₂ inch thick)
¹/₃ cup hot coffee

¹/₂ teaspoon sugar
1 tablespoon cream
Splash bourbon

1. Melt the butter in a heavy 12-inch skillet over high heat. Quickly sauté the ham on both sides until lightly browned.

2. Combine the remaining ingredients and pour over the ham. Cook over medium heat, turning once, for about 5 minutes.

SERVES 2

❋

NATIONAL HUNTING AND FISHING DAY— FOURTH SATURDAY IN SEPTEMBER

NATIONAL HUNTING AND FISHING DAY was established by presidential proclamation in 1979 by President Jimmy Carter, not in recognition of the sports themselves, but rather as a proclamation of appreciation for the sound and responsible environmental principles that the majority of hunters and fishermen hold dear. Since I am not a hunter, we'll just celebrate the occasion with a fish recipe.

▪ PAN-FRIED TROUT ▪

I liked going fishing with my father when I was a youngster. Although I dreaded getting up before dawn, it was exciting to go traipsing to out-of-the-way places, where only beavers lived and built their dams. The fish we caught we brought home for my mother to cook. More often than not, there was plenty for everyone.

4 brook or rainbow trout (8 to 12 ounces each), pan dressed (cleaned with head removed)
½ cup all-purpose flour

½ teaspoon salt
2 tablespoons unsalted butter
2 tablespoons vegetable oil
Lemon wedges

1. Pat the fish dry and dredge with flour. Sprinkle with salt.

2. Heat the butter and oil in a large heavy skillet until hot but not smoking. Sauté the fish over medium heat until crisp and firm, 3 to 4 minutes per side.

SERVES 4

✻

ALLIGATOR FESTIVAL—LAST FULL
WEEKEND IN SEPTEMBER

IF YOU HAVE   a taste for fried alligator, head to Boutte, Louisiana, where you can also sample 'gator po' boys, 'gator burgers, and grilled 'gator tails. Among the more exciting events at this festival are the 'gator races and the alligator beauty pageant—you get to pick the winner. For more information, contact the Rotary Club of St. Charles Parish at (504) 785-6242.

■ GRILLED ALLIGATOR TAIL ■

They say that the tenderest 'gators are those that come in under three feet. Cut the skin from the tail and cut the tail into strips. Marinate the meat in lemon juice for several hours. Wipe dry and place on a hot grill. Turn the meat often, basting with bacon drippings and Worcestershire sauce, until done. The time depends on the size of the strips, but the meat should be treated like London broil (i.e., not cooked to death).

■ OCTOBER ■

A haze on the far horizon,
The infinite, tender sky,
The ripe rich tint of the cornfields,
And the wild geese sailing high—
And all over upland and lowland
The charms of the goldenrod—
Some of us call it Autumn,
And others call it God.

—WILL HEREBERT CARRUTH,
"EACH IN HIS OWN TONGUE,"
POEMS, 1908

October, as its name implies, was the eighth month of the Roman calendar. When the year was changed from ten months to twelve, numerous attempts to change the name of the month in honor of various famous Romans failed. October is generally the month of the first frost and the first snowfall—and with the exception of the most northern reaches of the country, the peak of the foliage season. In early New England, when the first snow flurries fell and the first frost dusted the ground in early October, it was known as "squaw winter." The warm period that generally followed was called "Indian summer." Both terms are still in use in the northern climates.

❊

INTERNATIONAL MICROWAVE MONTH: Sponsored by Campbell Microwave Institute, of soup company fame, to promote the use of microwave ovens.

NATIONAL APPLE MONTH: Sponsored by the apple industry to promote and celebrate the year's harvest.

NATIONAL APPLE JACK MONTH: Sponsored by Laird's Apple Jack to celebrate "America's oldest native distilled spirit."

NATIONAL PIZZA MONTH: Sponsored by *Pizza Today* magazine to promote the "nutritional" values of "America's Number One Fun Food."

NATIONAL POPCORN POPPIN' MONTH: Sponsored by the Popcorn Institute to celebrate America's favorite healthy snack food.

NATIONAL SEAFOOD MONTH: Sponsored by the National Fisheries Institute to provide consumers with information regarding the nutritional values and varieties of fish and shellfish.

VEGETARIAN AWARENESS MONTH: Sponsored by VEGANET (Vegetarian Awareness Network) to promote an ethical, healthful, humane, and economical lifestyle.

AMERICAN BEER WEEK: Sponsored by the Association of Brewers to celebrate America's booming beer industry. More than 300 local and national beers are featured at the "Great American Beer Fest."

NATIONAL PICKLED PEPPER WEEK: Sponsored by Pickle Packers International, Inc., to celebrate bell, banana, cherry, chile, and other peppers of the "pickling" variety.

THIS TWO-DAY FEST, which takes place just south of Santa Barbara, California, in Carpinteria, honors this seaside town's most important crop. It includes "an appetizing array of foods, treasures, and other pleasures . . ." including lots of "guac 'n' roll" and a special screening of the riveting *Cannibal Women in the Avocado Jungle of Death.* And when the stomach growls, there are, aside from every variation of guacamole imaginable and the ubiquitous tamales and tacos, unusual offerings such as fettuccine with avocado, seviche with avocado, avocado cheesecake, avocado brownies, and avocado ice cream. For more information, contact the California Avocado Festival at (805) 684-0038.

▪ FETTUCCINE WITH WALNUTS AND AVOCADO ▪

This recipe, sent to me by the festival committee, makes a wonderful brunch dish. I sometimes omit the nuts and toss in some chopped smoked salmon. Leftover grilled fresh tuna or swordfish would also be wonderful additions.

2 tablespoons olive oil
1/4 cup sherry wine vinegar
1/3 cup diced sun-dried tomatoes
1/2 cup chopped fresh basil
2 scallions, chopped

1/4 cup diced green bell pepper
2 tablespoons chopped walnuts
1 avocado, peeled and diced
1 1/4 pounds dry fettuccine

1. In a large bowl, combine all the ingredients except the fettuccine and toss well.

2. Cook the pasta in boiling water until just tender. Drain well. Add to the bowl and toss while the pasta is still hot. Serve immediately.

SERVES 6

IF YOU ARE a fan of the seafood that the Northwest has to offer, this festival in Shelton, Washington, is for you. Fresh oysters, clams, mussels, salmon, and crab— they're all here. You can sample plain-old wonderful chowder, steamed clams, clam sandwiches, and an old-fashioned salmon bake, or you can opt for "gourmet" oyster dishes prepared by local chefs. The festival is educational, as well. You can learn all about the Northwest and the fishing industry during the breaks you'll need from dancing to fifties' rock and roll. The climax? Sunday's oyster-shucking contest to determine the West Coast champion. For more information, contact the Washington State Seafood Festival at (206) 426-2021.

▪ THE BEST-EVER CRAB DIP ▪

This crab dip was a best-seller at The Store in Amagansett many years ago. I still make it and serve it with crudités, but sadly, I can no longer enjoy the dip myself, as I am now allergic to crab.

8 ounces cream cheese, at room
   temperature
1 package (6 ounces) frozen king
   crabmeat, thawed and chopped
3 shallots, minced
1 teaspoon beef bouillon powder
   (optional)

1/4 cup sour cream
1 cup mayonnaise
1/2 teaspoon hot pepper sauce
1/2 cup chopped fresh dill
Salt to taste

Beat the cream cheese in a large bowl until light. Beat in the remaining ingredients until smooth. Refrigerate, covered, until well chilled.

MAKES ABOUT 2 1/2 CUPS

APPLE HARVEST FESTIVAL—FIRST TWO WEEKENDS IN OCTOBER

ONE OF THE NICEST and most popular apple festivals in the Northeast takes place in Southington, Connecticut. Some 350,000 people attend this annual event, which begins the weekend before Columbus Day and climaxes on Columbus Day itself. (Some years the festivity actually begins in September.) There are the usual arts-and-crafts displays and a parade that features high school bands from the region. There's a talent showcase, comedy, concerts, dances, and races of all sorts—including bed races. If you want to enter your bed, it must have four wheels and a rider. Other than that, anything goes. The race, a block long, is against the clock. Food booths are staffed by local civic and church groups and offer such apple goodies as cider, fritters, sundaes, caramel apples, candied apples, apple pie, apple crisp, apple strudel, and fried apple rings. For more information, contact the Greater Southington Chamber of Commerce at (203) 628-8036.

SOUTHINGTON Apple HARVEST FESTIVAL

▪ APPLE STRUDEL ▪

Apple strudel is one of my favorite apple desserts. The apricot preserves make this version a bit unusual. Commercial strudel (phyllo) leaves are perfectly acceptable. Buy them fresh, if possible. Frozen leaves must be defrosted before using.

²/₃ cup apricot preserves

3 tablespoons orange juice

²/₃ cup plus 2 teaspoons sugar

3 tart green apples (about 1 pound), cut into thin slices

6 strudel leaves

6 tablespoons (³/₄ stick) unsalted butter, melted (approximately)

3 tablespoons white bread crumbs

1¹/₂ teaspoons ground cinnamon

¹/₃ cup golden raisins

¹/₃ cup coarsely chopped walnuts

1. Preheat the oven to 375° F. In a small saucepan, combine the apricot preserves with the orange juice and ²/₃ cup sugar. Stir over medium heat until the sugar dissolves. Remove from the heat and cool.

2. Combine the apple slices with about half the apricot mixture. Toss to moisten the apples.

3. Place two strudel leaves on a sheet of waxed paper that rests on a damp tea towel. (The long side should be parallel to the edge of the table.) Brush the top leaf with melted butter; sprinkle with half the bread crumbs. Add another two leaves of dough. Brush again with butter and sprinkle with bread crumbs. Add two more leaves and brush with butter.

4. Spread the remaining apricot mixture over the top two-thirds of the dough. Arrange the apples over the bottom third, leaving an inch all around the edges of the dough. Sprinkle apples with cinnamon, raisins, and walnuts. With the aid of the towel, fold the side edges of the dough toward the center just enough to cover the filling by ¹/₂ inch. Brush the edges with butter and press lightly so they do not unfold.

5. With the aid of the towel, roll up the dough away from you and place it on a lightly buttered baking sheet. Brush the surface of the dough with butter and sprinkle with the remaining sugar. Bake until crisp, about 30 minutes. Slide onto a rack to cool. Serve slightly warm, with whipped cream or softened vanilla ice cream.

SERVES 6

✳

LEIF ERIKSSON DAY — OCTOBER 9

NORWEGIANS CAN TAKE HEART. Archaeological evidence of Norse presence in the New World has turned up at L'Anse aux Meadows on the northern tip of Newfoundland. So it seems that Leif Eriksson did, after all, discover America. Or did he? According to anthropologist Samuel M. Wilson in an article he wrote for *Natural History,* Eriksson was second. It was another Norseman, Bjarni Herjolfsson, who arrived here first. Quoting from *The Norse Atlantic Saga* (translated by Gwen Jones, Oxford University Press, 1986), Wilson states that Herjolfsson accidentally discovered North America about a thousand years ago when he was blown off course by a fierce storm. But since he was actually looking for Greenland, he made no attempts to land here. He related his discovery, however, to Leif, son of Erik the Red. Leif set sail and dubbed the new land "Vinland"—and in the process, received all the credit. Later, his brother, Thorvald, made the trip, and encountering native peoples, killed them. In return, Thorvald and crew were attacked and Thorvald was killed. Even so, the question remains as to why the Norsemen made no attempts at colonization. It has been speculated that because of native hostility, Norse internal disagreements, and the distance from Europe, any such attempt would have been doomed. It might also be that the time was not ripe for European involvement and discovery. It would be almost five hundred years before Columbus would sail into the Caribbean. Though there may be a Herjolfsson Day on future calendars, Eriksson was the first Norseman to *set foot* on the new land.

Though Leif Eriksson Day was celebrated in some areas before 1964, it was in that year, after much lobbying by Norwegians, that October 9 was established by presidential proclamation as the official day on which we celebrate the occasion. October 9 was selected because it was on that date in 1825 that the first large group of Norwegians arrived in America. (Some say that the Norwegians picked that day to divert attention from Columbus Day.)

▪ NORWEGIAN BEEF STEW ▪

One of the most famous Norwegian Americans was Hubert Humphrey, vice president under Lyndon Johnson. The recipe that follows is a version of a Norwegian soup that is reported to be an original invention of his widow, Muriel Humphrey Brown.

3 tablespoons vegetable oil
1½ pounds beef round, cut into ¾-inch
  cubes
1 medium onion, chopped
2 cups beef broth (approximately)
1 can (14 ounces) plum tomatoes with
  juices, chopped
2 medium ribs celery, chopped
  (about 1 cup)
4 medium carrots, cut into ½-inch-thick
  slices (about 2 cups)

1¼ cups chopped cabbage
  (about ¼ pound)
1 tablespoon Worcestershire sauce
1 large bay leaf
Pinch dried oregano
1 medium potato, peeled and
  cut into ½-inch cubes
Salt and freshly ground pepper
Chopped fresh parsley

1. Heat the oil in a medium pot over medium heat until hot. Sauté the beef, in two batches, until well browned, about 15 minutes altogether. Transfer to a plate.

2. Add the onion to the pot and cook, stirring constantly, for 2 minutes. Return the meat and stir in the broth, scraping the sides and bottom of the pot with a wooden spoon. Heat to boiling, skimming the surface as needed. Add the tomato, celery, carrot, cabbage, Worcestershire sauce, bay leaf, and oregano. Simmer, covered, skimming the surface occasionally, for 1½ hours.

3. Add the potato to the stew and continue to simmer, covered, for 30 minutes. (Add more broth if the stew becomes too thick.)

4. Discard the bay leaf, add salt and pepper to taste, and serve, sprinkled with parsley.

SERVES 4

THIS FESTIVAL in Chincoteague, on Virginia's eastern shore, is neither big nor fancy. In fact, it is held in a campground. It is a must, however, if you are an oyster lover. Indeed, many oyster aficionados believe that Chincoteague oysters are the absolute cream of the oyster crop. Believe it or not, there are only about 1,650 tickets available to this all-you-can-eat, four-hour affair, so call ahead (see below) and call early. Diehards head straight for the raw oysters, but you can also get oyster stew, oyster fritters, and fried oysters. Because of the time limit, a somewhat frenzied air hangs over the place. It seems as if you can never get enough! For more information, contact the Chincoteague Chamber of Commerce at (800) 446-8038.

▪ OYSTERS ON THE HALF SHELL ▪

If you are lucky enough to have Chincoteagues on hand, by all means use them. Other good oysters for the half shell include Grand Isles, Apalachicolas, Cotuits, and Bluepoints.

6 to 8 oysters per person	Lemon wedges
1 tablespoon cornstarch	Hot pepper sauce

1. Scrub the oysters and place them in a large pot of cold water to which you have added the cornstarch. Let them soak for 30 minutes. Rinse well.

2. To open an oyster, hold it firmly in one hand and push the blade of an oyster knife between the shells near the hinge. Work the knife around the oyster until you feel it loosen. Force the top shell up.

3. If you should damage the shells while opening, strain the juices through cheesecloth and pour them back over the oyster. Serve on a bed of crushed ice, accompanied by lemon wedges and hot sauce.

In fourteen hundred and ninety-two,
Columbus sailed the ocean blue.

IF ALL HISTORY lessons were taught in such catchy phrases, we would retain a lot more knowledge than we do. And even if, as kids, we couldn't exactly grasp the abstract idea of the discovery of the New World (most of us hadn't even come to grips with the Old), we remembered that date. Likewise, the lyrical names of Columbus's ships—the *Niña,* the *Pinta,* and the *Santa Maria*—just rolled off our tongues.

Much has been written about Columbus and his arrival in the New World on the twelfth of October. Five hundred years after his famous voyage, controversy abounds. And although his exploits were minor in comparison with those of some explorers that followed, it was Columbus who eventually became the symbol of the New World's discovery. Nowadays, we look long and hard at the atrocities committed in the name of that "discovery," but we cannot ignore the impact of the event on the foodways of the world. Tomatoes, potatoes, corn, peppers, squash, and cocoa found their way to the Old World. Cattle, pigs, horses, sugar, citrus fruits and figs, and olives entered the New.

The anniversary of Columbus's landing wasn't even celebrated until 1792, three hundred years after his voyage. The first celebration was held in New York City by the Society of St. Tammany, also called the Columbian Order. It wasn't until a century later that October 12 was proclaimed a legal holiday by President Benjamin Harrison. Another proclamation was issued by President Franklin Delano Roosevelt in 1937, designating October 12 as Columbus Day. Since 1971 the holiday has been observed on the second Monday of October.

Though Columbus claimed his discoveries in the name of Spain, he was a native of Genoa, Italy. Consequently, Columbus Day is celebrated by Italian-Americans from coast to coast.

▪ ANNA TERESA CALLEN'S ▪
INCREDIBLE LASAGNA

Anna Teresa Callen, an extremely talented cooking teacher and respected author, comes from Abruzzi—quite a jog from Genoa. But if you want to serve an Italian brunch dish on Columbus Day, you can't do better than this remarkable lasagna.

Bolognese Sauce (recipe follows)

¼ cup chopped cooked spinach

2 eggs

Pinch salt

2 cups all-purpose flour (approximately)

8 ounces mozzarella, coarsely grated

1 cup freshly grated Parmesan

Besciamella Sauce (recipe follows)

2 tablespoons unsalted butter

3 tablespoons freshly grated Parmesan

1. Prepare the Bolognese Sauce.

2. *To make the pasta dough:* In a food processor fitted with the steel blade, process the spinach for 5 seconds. Add the eggs and salt. With the machine running, slowly add 1½ cups flour through the feed tube. Add more flour, 1 tablespoon at a time, until a smooth ball is formed. Transfer the dough to a lightly floured board. Knead for 5 minutes. Cover; let stand for 30 minutes.

3. Roll out the pasta dough as thin as possible, either by hand, or using a pasta machine; add more flour if the dough seems sticky. Cut the dough into strips, 9 inches long and 2½ inches wide. (The size can be adjusted to fit the dish you are using.)

4. Heat 4 quarts of water to boiling. Add the lasagna noodles, a few at a time; boil for 3 minutes. Remove to a damp towel; cover while cooking the remaining pasta.

5. Spread 2 tablespoons of Bolognese Sauce over the bottom of a lasagna pan or a 2½-quart ovenproof baking dish. Add a layer of noodles. Spread the noodles with a thin layer of Bolognese Sauce. Sprinkle with mozzarella and Parmesan. Continue layering, ending up with sauce and cheese, until all of the sauce and cheese is used up. (If you have rolled the pasta thin enough, there should be excess for the freezer. To freeze uncooked pasta, cut a piece of cardboard to fit inside a large resealable plastic bag. Cover the cardboard with wax paper and layer the leftover noodles between layers of wax paper. Slip into bag, seal, and freeze.)

6. Preheat the oven to 375° F. Make the Besciamella Sauce.

7. Spoon the sauce over the top of the prepared lasagna. Gently push in the sides to allow the sauce to run down. Dot with butter; sprinkle with the 3 tablespoons Parmesan. Bake for 45 minutes, or until lightly browned and bubbly. Let stand for 10 minutes before serving.

SERVES 6 TO 8

N O T E : This dish can be prepared in advance through step 5 and refrigerated. Let stand at room temperature for 30 minutes before continuing.

BOLOGNESE SAUCE

3 tablespoons olive oil
1 tablespoon unsalted butter
4 ounces prosciutto (end piece is fine), finely chopped
1 medium onion, finely chopped
1 medium carrot, finely chopped
1 stalk celery, finely chopped
1 sprig parsley, finely chopped
1 pound ground meat (beef, veal, and pork in equal portions)
3 chopped sage leaves
1/4 cup dry white wine
3 tablespoons tomato paste
2 cups chicken broth
1/4 cup heavy cream
Salt and freshly ground pepper

1. Heat the oil and butter in a medium saucepan over medium heat. Sauté the prosciutto, onion, carrot, and celery until lightly browned. Add the parsley and ground meats. Cook over high heat, breaking up lumps of meat, until the meat is well browned. Reduce the heat.

2. Add the sage, wine, tomato paste, and broth to the saucepan. Simmer, covered, over medium-low heat for 1 hour. Stir in the cream; add salt and pepper to taste.

MAKES ABOUT 4 CUPS

BESCIAMELLA SAUCE

2½ tablespoons unsalted butter
2½ tablespoons all-purpose flour
2½ cups milk
Salt
Freshly grated nutmeg

Melt the butter in a small saucepan over medium-low heat. Stir in the flour. Cook, stirring constantly, for 2 minutes. Add the milk all at once and beat until smooth. Heat to boiling over medium-low heat. Allow the sauce to "puff" two or three times; remove from the heat. Add salt and nutmeg to taste.

MAKES ABOUT 2½ CUPS

✳

OHIO SAUERKRAUT FESTIVAL—
SECOND WEEKEND IN OCTOBER

YOU MIGHT THINK that sauerkraut is a peculiar item to build a festival around, but in Waynesville, Ohio, that's just what they do. While the festival features more than 300 arts-and-crafts booths, you'll be kept busy just tasting all the sauerkraut offerings. Try sloppy kraut in pita for starters. Then move on to kraut pizza and a Reuben sandwich. For dessert try sauerkraut chocolate cake and kraut cookies. This festival's attendance runs around 200,000, which just proves that there are a lot of kraut lovers out there. For more information, contact the Waynesville Area Chamber of Commerce at (513) 897-8855.

▪ REUBEN SANDWICH ▪

The Reuben sandwich is said to have been named for Arthur Reuben, who supposedly invented it at his delicatessen in New York City, which was also called Reuben's, way back in 1914. That's one story. Two others involve Omaha. One version has a deli owner by the name of Reuben Kulakofsky inventing it in the 1930s. Another has an Omaha grocer named Reuben Kay inventing it during a poker game in 1955. Legend has it that it was so good, someone entered it in a contest—and the rest is history.

¼ cup mayonnaise
1 teaspoon minced green bell pepper
1½ teaspoons chile sauce
4 slices rye bread
4 bread-sized slices Swiss cheese

¼ pound sliced corned beef
½ cup sauerkraut, well-drained
2 tablespoons unsalted butter
  (approximately)

1. In a small bowl, combine the mayonnaise, green pepper, and chili sauce. Spread about 1 tablespoon of the mixture over each slice of bread. Place a piece of cheese on each slice of bread. Place half the corned beef on one slice; then place half the sauerkraut on top. Cover with one slice prepared bread, cheese side down. Make the other sandwich in the same manner.

2. Melt the butter in a heavy skillet over medium heat. Brown the sandwiches on one side, then turn them over and brown them on the other side, adding more butter if needed, and making sure the cheese melts.

SERVES 2

＊

WEST VIRGINIA BLACK WALNUT FESTIVAL— SECOND WEEKEND IN OCTOBER

WHEN IT COMES to walnuts, many feel that the absolute finest are native American black walnuts. To sample them at their best, take a drive to Spencer, West Virginia, about sixty miles northeast of Charleston, high in the scenic Appalachian Mountains. Here you'll find entertainment—canoe races, chicken-flying contests, banjo picking, clogging, arm wrestling, and more; bake sales, featuring cakes, cupcakes, fudge, brownies, and pies—all made with black walnuts, of course; and a cooking contest, usually centered around a theme, such as brownies. For more information, contact the West Virginia Black Walnut Festival at (304) 927-3708.

▪ BLACK-WALNUT BROWNIES ▪

These are my favorite brownies. They could win a contest any day—and make lovely Christmas presents boxed in a pretty tin.

2 ounces unsweetened chocolate
½ cup (1 stick) unsalted butter, cut into pieces
2 large eggs
1 cup sugar

1 teaspoon vanilla extract
½ cup all-purpose flour
Pinch salt
¼ cup sour cream
½ to ⅔ cup chopped black walnuts

1. Preheat the oven to 325° F. Grease an 8-inch square cake pan.

2. Melt the chocolate with the butter in the top of a double boiler over hot water until smooth. Cool slightly.

3. In a large bowl, beat the eggs with the sugar until light. Slowly beat in the chocolate mixture. Stir in the vanilla. Sift in the flour, 2 tablespoons at a time, mixing well after each addition. Stir in the salt, sour cream, and walnuts.

4. Pour the batter into the prepared pan. Bake until a toothpick inserted in the center comes out fairly clean, about 25 to 30 minutes. The center should be slightly cakey. Cool completely on a wire rack before cutting into bars.

MAKES ABOUT 20 BROWNIES

EVERY YEAR a party is held in Santa Cruz, California, the "Sprout Capital of the World" . . . "to gain some respect for poor Brussels sprouts." The festivities start with a parade and the naming of the Brussels Sprouts Queen. There are people in Santa Cruz who remember clearly when a young woman named Norma Jean Dougherty won that crown in 1947. There are cooking demonstrations as well, so you'll know what to do with your sprouts when you take some home. Join in the sprout toss, or sample sprouts tempura, marinated sprouts, sprout pizza, and, if you dare, sprout water taffy and sprout ice cream. Oh, yes! You can even win a trip for two. Where to? Why, Brussels (Belgium), of course. For more information, contact the Santa Cruz Beach Boardwalk at (408) 423-5590.

■ MARINATED BRUSSELS SPROUTS ■

1 cup water
½ cup olive oil
¼ cup lemon juice
1 medium white onion, halved and
thinly sliced
1 pound Brussels sprouts, trimmed, an
X cut in each root end

1 teaspoon chopped fresh tarragon
2 teaspoons white-wine vinegar
Salt and freshly ground pepper
Chopped fresh parsley

1. In a medium saucepan, combine the water, oil, and lemon juice. Heat to boiling; reduce the heat and simmer, uncovered, for 10 minutes.

2. Add the onion slices and sprouts to the saucepan. Return to boiling; reduce the heat and simmer, uncovered, until barely tender, about 10 minutes. Remove from the heat and let cool in the liquid.

3. Transfer the mixture, including the liquid, to a serving dish. Add the tarragon, vinegar, and salt and pepper to taste. Chill thoroughly before serving, garnished with parsley.

SERVES 4 TO 6

■ WORLD FOOD DAY—OCTOBER 16 ■

World Food Day was established in 1981 by the United Nations' Food and Agriculture Organization, on the anniversary of its founding (1945), to heighten public awareness of farm, food, health, and hunger issues. In the United States, an independent, nonprofit umbrella organization has been set up to coordinate various activities that take place not only on October 16, but all year round. The work is supported by donations from member organizations. One of the feature events of the 16th is a worldwide satellite teleconference that links concerned and committed people from all corners of the earth. There are many local fund-raising drives, educational programs, and lectures, as well. Most local affairs are covered in regional newspapers. For information on the national picture, contact the National Committee for World Food Day at (202) 653-2404.

*

CIRCLEVILLE PUMPKIN SHOW—
THIRD WEDNESDAY IN OCTOBER

"THE GREATEST FREE SHOW ON EARTH" is what they call the Circleville Pumpkin Show in Circleville, Ohio—one of the largest annual festivals and agricultural exhibits in the United States. Every year, approximately 500,000 people show up to partake in the fun. During this four-day event there are seven parades, including one for Little Miss Pumpkins, one for Miss Pumpkins, one for Baby Pumpkins, and even one for the Pumpkins' pets. There is a midway, entertainment galore, and plenty of pumpkins. In fact, the traditional display of pumpkins stands about 15 feet tall and weighs more than 100,000 pounds. That's a lot of pie filling! Speaking of which, the folks at Circleville also claim to make the world's biggest pie —5 feet across and weighing in at 350 pounds. The food booths feature such intriguing items as doughnuts, waffles, pancakes, fudge, taffy, fried chips, burgers, sloppy Joes, and soda—every single one of which is made with pumpkin. For more information, contact the Circleville Pumpkin Show at (614) 474-4923.

▪ PUMPKIN COOKIES ▪

This recipe comes from a 92-page pamphlet that is simply called Pumpkin Recipes *and is compiled by the Crusader Sunday School Class at Calvary United Methodist Church. For a copy, write Crusaders Class, P.O. Box 8, Circleville, Ohio 43113.*

⅓ cup vegetable shortening or unsalted
   butter, at room temperature
1⅓ cups sugar
2 eggs
1 cup canned solid-pack pumpkin
1 teaspoon vanilla extract
1 teaspoon lemon juice
1 teaspoon finely grated lemon zest
2½ cups sifted all-purpose flour

4 teaspoons baking powder
1 teaspoon salt
¼ teaspoon ground ginger
¼ teaspoon ground allspice
1 teaspoon ground nutmeg
1 teaspoon ground cinnamon
1 cup raisins
½ cup chopped nuts

1. Preheat the oven to 400° F. In a large mixing bowl, beat the shortening until light. Slowly beat in the sugar and then beat until light. Beat in the eggs, one at a time, and then beat in the pumpkin, vanilla, lemon juice, and lemon zest.

2. Sift the dry ingredients together and slowly stir into the cookie batter. Stir in the raisins and nuts.

3. Drop the batter by teaspoonfuls onto lightly greased cookie sheets. (They spread very little.) Bake until lightly browned, 15 to 18 minutes. Cool on wire racks.

MAKES ABOUT 4 ½ DOZEN

✳

DIWALI (DEWALI) —
OCTOBER OR NOVEMBER

THE WORD *diwali* means "cluster of lights." Diwali is the most important Hindu festival, and is sometimes compared to Christmas in the Christian world. This seven-day festival heralds the beginning of the Hindu New Year. It is also a celebration of the return of Shri Ram (God incarnate) after a fourteen-year exile, and his victory over the demon ruler Ravana. The day celebrates light over darkness, good over evil. On the seventh day, families get together and exchange gifts of sweets, dried fruits, nuts, and nowadays, new clothes. The meal is generally vegetarian. Each diner receives four or five little cups, called *katoris,* containing separate dishes. These dishes are usually accompanied by the Indian breads *poori* and *papadum.*

▪ GARLICKY BRAISED EGGPLANT ▪

The following recipe is inspired by a spicy hot eggplant dish invented by Julie Sahni. Mine is much tamer. Her version, in the classic Classic Indian Vegetarian and Grain Cooking *(William Morrow, 1985), not only uses "4 to 8" hot green chiles, but cayenne pepper as well. Julie, who is one of the most remarkable women in the food business, notes that all you need to complete a meal is a simple lentil puree* (dal) *and some cooked rice.*

1 medium eggplant (about 1 pound)
⅓ cup peanut (or mustard) oil
3 large cloves garlic, sliced
1 large onion, halved and thinly sliced
1 hot green chile pepper, seeded,
   deveined, and sliced

1 medium baking potato (½ pound),
   halved lengthwise and cut across into
   ¼-inch-thick slices
½ teaspoon ground turmeric
2 medium tomatoes, peeled, seeded,
   and chopped
Salt and freshly ground pepper to taste

1. Trim the ends off the eggplant. Cut in half lengthwise and then cut each half across into ½-inch-thick slices. Place in a large bowl and cover with cold water. Let stand 30 minutes. Drain and pat dry.

2. Heat the oil in a large, deep, heavy skillet until very hot. Add the garlic and cook 30 seconds. Add the onion slices and cook, tossing very carefully, until the onions begin to turn golden, about 4 to 5 minutes. Reduce heat to medium-high if garlic begins to burn.

3. Add the chile pepper and potato to the onion mixture. Cook, tossing gently, 2 minutes. Toss in the eggplant and sprinkle with turmeric. Continue to cook, tossing gently, until eggplant begins to soften, about 3 minutes. Reduce heat to medium and stir in the tomatoes. Continue to cook, stirring occasionally, until vegetables are tender, 12 to 15 minutes longer. Add salt and pepper to taste.

SERVES 4 TO 6

✻

LEXINGTON, NORTH CAROLINA, is famous for its barbecue, considered by many barbecue aficionados to be the world's best. The fare is pork, of course—and shoulder is the cut of choice in Lexington. It is slowly cooked and basted over hickory wood until it is fall-apart tender. The meat is served chopped, not sliced, with more of the basting, or "moppin'," sauce on the side. The sauce is vinegar-based, rather than the sweet tomato (read catsup) sauce used elsewhere. There are events during the day: a Parade of Pigs (featuring people dressed up as such), a hog-calling contest, gospel singing, square dancing, and more. But people really come to eat barbecue. So, opt for a barbecue platter with coleslaw and hush puppies. Or just grab a sandwich with (traditional) or without coleslaw on it. 'Tis a great day for barbecue lovers. For more information, contact the Lexington Barbecue Festival at (704) 243-2629.

▪ NORTH CAROLINA MOPPIN' SAUCE ▪

While this vinegary sauce is meant to be used for moppin', on occasion it's used for dippin' as well. Serve it with pork, needless to say.

1½ cups cider vinegar
1 tablespoon dry mustard
2 teaspoons cayenne

1 tablespoon Worcestershire sauce
1 tablespoon vegetable oil

Combine all of the ingredients in a medium saucepan. Slowly heat to just below boiling. Let cool for 2 hours.

MAKES ABOUT 1 ½ CUPS

✳

HALLOWEEN — OCTOBER 31

ALTHOUGH IT MAY well stem from an old European custom of the poor begging for "soul-cakes" on All Souls' Day (November 2), "trick-or-treating" is an American phenomenon, and a fairly recent one at that. Children dressed up in costumes, going from door to door with a paper bag, was unheard of in many parts of the country until the 1950s. Getting into mischief, however, is another matter completely. This behavior can be traced to pagan times. All Hallows' Day, or All Saints' Day, falls on November 1. By tradition, the celebration begins at sundown on the preceding day. It is the festival of the dead, the night on which ghosts and dead souls make their annual appearance. It is a night for pranks—soaping windows, throwing eggs, and sometimes a lot worse.

In more innocent times, the highlight of a Halloween party was bobbing for apples. Some believe the custom stems from Celtic ceremonies in which apples were used to select a lover. In parts of the South, folklore has it that if you can break an apple in half with your bare hands, or eat a crab apple without frowning, you will get the spouse of your choice. But there seems to be no specific tie-in between apple-bobbing and Halloween other than the simple fact that Halloween is a fall festival and apples are therefore plentiful. The pumpkin, the other food specifically tied to Halloween, is, of course, a New World discovery. In the Old World, jack-o'-lanterns were most often carved out of large turnips. The candle-lit face was said to frighten witches and ghosts.

Halloween is not just for kids, either. Adults have long been going to costume parties, but in the 1970s the costume parties began taking to the streets. What started ostensibly as Gay Mardi Gras–style parades in such cities as New York, San Francisco, Atlanta, and elsewhere, have grown into major celebrations enjoyed by all.

▪ GHOULISH GRUEL ▪

While this is actually nothing more than a pineapple-grapefruit drink, the addition of some red or blue food coloring will make it truly ghoulish. Or try peeling some grapes and putting them in each glass, along with a drop of soda. There's nothing in the world quite like an "eyeball fizz."

⅓ cup sugar

½ cup water

1¼ cups grapefruit juice

1 cup pineapple juice

¼ cup lemon juice

1. In a medium saucepan, combine the sugar with the water. Heat to boiling, reduce the heat, and simmer for 4 minutes. Cool.
2. Add the remaining ingredients to the cooled syrup. Chill thoroughly.

SERVES 3 OR 4

■ NOVEMBER ■

Yet one smile more, departing, distant sun!
One mellow smile through the soft vapory air,
E're o'er the frozen earth, the loud winds run,
Or snows are sifted o'er the meadows bare.

—WILLIAM CULLEN BRYANT,
"NOVEMBER" 1824

Like September and October, November retained its name when it was moved from ninth place to eleventh on the expanded twelve-month calendar. At one point, however, the Roman senate attempted to rename the month in honor of the second emperor Tiberius, who just happened to have been born in November. He refused the honor, wondering what would happen to the calendar if every ruler had a month of the year named after him—and after all, there are only twelve months in the year. The Saxons called the month *Windmonath,* a reference to the furious winds that forced fishing boats from the seas.

❋

✳

LOUISIANA PECAN FESTIVAL—
FIRST WEEKEND IN NOVEMBER

COLFAX is the county seat of Grant Parish, Louisiana, and home to the Louisiana Pecan Festival. The yearly pecan recipe contest is held on Friday, the first day of this three-day event. Homemade pecan pies, cookies, cakes, and other goodies are sold at the country store during the festival. You can also buy pecans by the sackful. They even have a clever little device that partially cracks the shells for you, which keeps them as fresh as possible and saves a lot of hard work at home. The most interesting aspect of this festival is that you can try varieties of pecans that never make it to the grocers' shelves. These include Schley, Cape Fear, Sly, Choctaw, and Candy—all superior to the Stuart, which retailers and shippers prefer because of its hardiness. For more information, contact the Louisiana Pecan Festival at (318) 627-3711.

■ THE BEST PECAN PIE ■

I have been making this pie for more than twenty years. I have tried a lot of pecan pie recipes, including ones with chocolate, but I still think this is the best of the bunch.

PASTRY
1½ cups all-purpose flour
¼ teaspoon salt
6 tablespoons (¾ stick) cold unsalted
   butter
2 tablespoons plus 1 teaspoon cold
   vegetable shortening
3 to 4 tablespoons cold water

FILLING
3 eggs

2 tablespoons unsalted butter, melted
2 tablespoons all-purpose flour
½ teaspoon vanilla extract
⅛ teaspoon salt
½ cup sugar
1½ cups dark corn syrup
1½ cups chopped pecans
½ cup unbroken pecan halves
   (approximately)
Unsweetened whipped cream

1. *To make the pastry:* In a large bowl, combine the flour with the salt. Cut in the butter and shortening with a knife and blend with a pastry blender until the mixture has the texture of coarse crumbs. Add the water, a tablespoon at a time, and mix gently with a fork to form a soft dough. Do not overwork. Refrigerate, covered, for 1 hour.

2. Preheat the oven to 425° F.

3. Roll out the pastry on a lightly floured board and line a 9-inch pie plate. Trim and flute the edges.

4. *To make the filling:* In a large bowl, beat the eggs until light. Whisk in the butter, flour, vanilla, salt, sugar, and syrup.

5. Sprinkle the chopped pecans over the bottom of the pastry shell. Gently pour the egg mixture over the pecans. Make a ring of unbroken pecan halves around the edge. Make another ring inside, and continue in this fashion until the surface is covered. Bake for 10 minutes. Reduce the oven temperature to 325° F and bake 40 minutes longer, or until nicely browned and a toothpick inserted in the center comes out clean. Let cool on a wire rack. Serve garnished with whipped cream, if desired.

SERVES 8

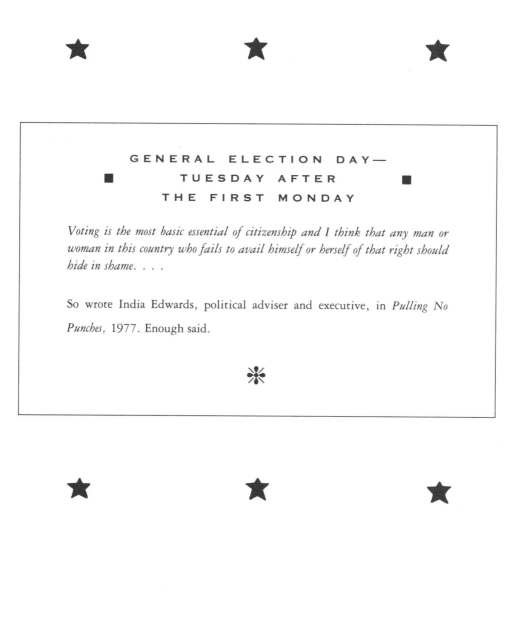

GENERAL ELECTION DAY— ■ TUESDAY AFTER ■ THE FIRST MONDAY

Voting is the most basic essential of citizenship and I think that any man or woman in this country who fails to avail himself or herself of that right should hide in shame. . . .

So wrote India Edwards, political adviser and executive, in *Pulling No Punches,* 1977. Enough said.

❋

✳

SANDWICH DAY—NOVEMBER 3

THIS DAY is actually the birthday of John Montague, fourth earl of Sandwich, who was born November 3, 1718. Though Montague spent much of his life in public service, he is just as renowned for his life as a gambler. He was reportedly partial to twenty-four-hour gambling marathons and invented the sandwich as a quick, nutritious form of sustenance that could easily be eaten without interrupting these sessions. The very first sandwiches, we have been told, were made with cold roast beef. It seems rather silly that someone actually got credit for throwing some leftover meat on bread, but so be it. Most of us grew up lugging sandwiches to school every day. Some of us have graduated from peanut butter–and–lettuce (on Wonder Bread) to BLTs, club sandwiches, and even po' boys.

▪ TURKEY CLUB SANDWICH ▪

Some say this sandwich got its name because it was first served in the club car of a train. Others say it was invented in the back of a casino (casinos were known as "clubs" at one time). Regardless of where the name came from, it's one of America's most popular sandwiches.

3 slices bread, toasted
Mayonnaise
2 to 3 crisp lettuce leaves
4 slices cooked turkey

Salt and freshly ground pepper
3 or 4 thin slices ripe tomato
3 or 4 slices crisp-fried bacon

Spread one side of each piece of toast with mayonnaise. Place the lettuce on one piece and top with turkey. Sprinkle with salt and pepper. Cover with the second piece of toast. Top that with the tomato and bacon (and more lettuce if you wish). Cover with the remaining piece of toast, mayonnaise side down. Insert toothpicks to keep the sandwich from falling apart and cut diagonally into quarters.

MAKES 1 SANDWICH

✳

BRAWLEY, in California's Imperial Valley, plays host to what is, in effect, a tribute to the cattle industry. It is attended by more than 50,000 cowboy and cowgirl wanna-bes—beef lovers all. The celebration features a beef cook-off, a rodeo, a western parade, western dances, and a bunch of Hollywood stars. Don't miss out on the chuck-wagon breakfast and the deep-pit beef barbecue. For more information, contact the Brawley Chamber of Commerce at (619) 344-3160.

▪ TROPICAL GRILLED FLANK STEAK ▪ WITH FRESH-FRUIT SALSA

The only beef cook-off that I have been invited to attend took place in Sun Valley, Idaho. It was 1987, the first year that barbecue was included as a category in the cook-off. This dish, invented by Debbie Vanni of Libertyville, Illinois, was the winner. Keep in mind that you must carve flank steak as soon as it comes off the heat. If you don't, the fibers will toughen as the meat cools. The salsa can be made in the morning and refrigerated until about half an hour before serving time.

1 beef flank steak (about 1½ pounds)
¼ cup fresh orange juice
2 tablespoons chili sauce
2 tablespoons soy sauce
2 tablespoons vegetable oil
1 teaspoon sugar
1 teaspoon grated orange peel

2 cloves garlic, minced
½ teaspoon salt
⅛ teaspoon hot pepper sauce
1 medium orange, thinly sliced
Fresh-Fruit Salsa (recipe follows)
Orange wedges
Fresh cilantro sprigs

1. Score both sides of the flank steak with a sharp knife in a diamond pattern. Place in a shallow glass or ceramic dish.

2. Combine the orange juice, chili sauce, soy sauce, vegetable oil, sugar, orange peel, garlic, salt, and hot pepper sauce. Pour over the meat. Lift the meat so both sides are coated. Place the orange slices over the meat. Cover tightly and refrigerate overnight. Let stand at room temperature about 1 hour before grilling.

3. Make the Fresh-Fruit Salsa.

4. Remove the steak from the marinade, and discard the marinade and orange slices. Broil the steak over medium heat, 3 to 5 minutes per side. Do not overcook. Flank steak is best served rare to medium-rare. Carve immediately on the diagonal into thin slices. Place on a platter and garnish with orange wedges and fresh cilantro. Serve with Fresh-fruit Salsa.

SERVES 4

FRESH-FRUIT SALSA

½ cup diced pineapple

½ cup diced mango

½ cup diced papaya

½ cup diced green apple

¼ cup diced red bell pepper

¼ cup diced green bell pepper

2 tablespoons white-wine vinegar

1 tablespoon minced fresh cilantro

4 teaspoons sugar

¼ teaspoon hot red pepper flakes

Combine all of the ingredients and mix well.

MAKES ABOUT 2½ CUPS

❋

✳

HOLIDAY FOLK FAIR—
WEEKEND BEFORE THANKSGIVING

THIS EVENT, sponsored by the International Institute of Wisconsin in Milwaukee, is the largest indoor ethnic event in the country. The purpose of the fair is to share the traditions of diverse ethnic groups. And though one group is highlighted each year, more than fifty regional ethnic groups participate. You might call this the "melting pot" festival. There are numerous cultural exhibits featuring customs, arts, music, dancing, etc. The big draw is the World Mart, where you can shop the world over, right down to the Old Delhi bazaar. At the Sidewalk Café, you can fill up on ethnic specialties from more than three dozen nationalities. Then head for the Coffeehouse to sample the various international desserts and coffees. For more information, contact the International Institute of Wisconsin's Holiday Folk Fair at (414) 933-0521.

▪ HUNGARIAN CHICKEN ▪

The Hungarians have a way with chicken, and this is one of my favorite dishes. Serve with buttered noodles.

2 small chickens (2½ pounds each),
   cut into pieces
Salt and freshly ground pepper
2 tablespoons vegetable oil
3 tablespoons unsalted butter
1 large yellow onion, finely chopped
1 rib celery, chopped
1 firm ripe tomato, chopped

2 tablespoons sweet Hungarian paprika
1 tablespoon tomato paste
1 cup hot chicken stock or broth
1 cup sour cream, at room temperature
2 teaspoons poppy seeds, toasted
   (see Note)
Chopped fresh parsley

1. Pat the chickens dry with paper towels. Sprinkle well with salt and pepper, rubbing the seasonings into the skin.

2. In a large heavy skillet or saucepan, heat the oil and 2 tablespoons of butter until hot. Sauté the chicken pieces, about half at a time, until well browned on both sides, about 5 minutes per side. Remove the chicken to a plate. Pour off all of the cooking fat.

3. Melt the remaining tablespoon of butter in the skillet and add the onion and celery. Cook, stirring constantly, for 3 minutes. Stir in the tomato and continue to stir, scraping the bottom and sides of the pan, for 2 minutes. Stir in the paprika, tomato paste, and chicken stock. Add the chicken, skin side down, and simmer, uncovered, for 30 minutes.

4. Turn the chicken over and continue to simmer, uncovered, basting frequently, until tender, 15 to 20 minutes longer. Transfer the chicken to a serving dish and keep warm.

5. Stir the sour cream into the chicken juices until thoroughly blended and warmed through. Do not allow to boil. Stir in the poppy seeds and pour over the chicken. Sprinkle with parsley.

SERVES 6

NOTE: To toast poppy seeds, lightly rub a nonstick skillet with butter or oil and place over medium heat until hot. Add poppy seeds and cook, stirring constantly, until seeds are heated through, about 1 minute.

✳

THANKSGIVING —
FOURTH THURSDAY IN NOVEMBER

THANKSGIVING, as we celebrate it today, is really based on a combination of past events. There is also the matter of semantics to be considered. The observance of the Pilgrims' first *harvest celebration* in 1621 is often portrayed as the first Thanksgiving, but that isn't quite so. There was indeed a harvest celebration—and it certainly was the Pilgrims' first. And yes, there was wild turkey and venison, games were played, and the Indians *were* guests. But it was not a day of giving thanks. Actually, the Pilgrims celebrated "thanksgiving" whenever life went well. When a day of thanksgiving was declared, it was in the name of God. All work virtually stopped, and everyone spent the day attending church services. These celebrations were very religious, somber affairs totally separate from the harvest celebration, which was strictly secular. As years went by, virtually every town and village in colonial America celebrated the harvest, in its own time and way. Later on, in 1769, the Pilgrim fathers came to be remembered on the anniversary of the *Mayflower's* landing, December 21. The holiday, Forefathers' Day, was a fairly important one until the late 1800s, when both the modern Thanksgiving and Christmas superseded it.

It was late in the nineteenth century that the romantic notion of the Pilgrims' first Thanksgiving (harvest, in this case) began to emerge. Ever since, erroneously or not, the Pilgrims have been very much a part of our Thanksgiving celebration. And while some of us still attend church services on Thanksgiving morning, the Pilgrims would be aghast to see us turn on the TV to watch the annual Detroit Lions game.

The first harvest celebration took place sometime between September 21 and November 9, according to *The Thanksgiving Primer,* a guide to re-creating the first harvest festival put out by the Plimoth Plantation, Inc. (The Plimoth Plantation is a "living museum of seventeenth-century Plymouth," whose exhibits are based on extensive ongoing research.) Actually, a great deal is written in the primer about the foods that were available to the Pilgrims. Wild turkey was most likely included, along with duck, goose, swan, and venison. Breads were skillet breads, made, most likely, of cornmeal. Herbs and salad ingredients grew wild, as did Jerusalem artichokes. Berries of all kinds "filled the gaps." Meals in those days were not served in courses. Rather, all the food was placed on the table at once. For history buffs, *The Thanksgiving Primer* can be ordered from Plimoth Plantation by calling (508) 746-1622.

George Washington proclaimed the first national Thanksgiving Day in 1789. Abraham Lincoln designated the last Thursday of the month as the official day—which made it very late if there happened to be five Thursdays. Franklin Roosevelt tried to make it the third Thursday to give retailers an extra week for Christmas sales, but that didn't sit well at all with the general public. Finally, in 1941, a Congressional Joint Resolution settled it once and for all, designating the fourth Thursday in November as Thanksgiving Day.

■ THE ANCIENT NEW ENGLAND STANDING DISH ■ OF POMPION

The Thanksgiving Primer *includes an intriguing recipe for "the Ancient New England Standing Dish of Pompion." This stewed pumpkin ("pompion") dish was standard (or "standing") for the time and was traditionally served with "Fish or Flesh."*

8 cups peeled diced pumpkin
¼ cup water
2 tablespoons unsalted butter
2 tablespoons vinegar

⅓ cup light brown sugar
¼ teaspoon ground ginger
¼ teaspoon ground cinnamon
Salt to taste

1. Place 2 cups of the pumpkin and ¼ cup of water in a pot and cook gently over very low heat until the pumpkin pieces sink down. Keep adding more pumpkin until you have used it all up. Do not add more water.

2. When the pumpkin is tender, add the remaining ingredients and stir gently to mix.

SERVES 6

✳

SINCE WORLD WAR II, the Friday after Thanksgiving, known as Black Friday, has traditionally marked the start of the Christmas shopping season. The term was supposedly coined by retailers in reference to the day that the ink on the ledgers turns from red to black. But in times of economic hardship, this day is a true test of retailers' nerves. How Black Friday goes, so goes the season. If it's a lackluster shopping day, expect a lot of Christmas "bargain sales" in the coming weeks. Traffic is notoriously snarled, so why not stay home and get started on the homemade Christmas presents that mean so much to family and friends?

▪ MELON JAM ▪

Honeydew melon is usually available year-round, even though it is known as a winter melon, and it makes excellent jam. If you've never given a gift of homemade jam, why not stay home today and give it a shot?

1 large or 2 small honeydew melons (about 5 pounds)
½ teaspoon grated lime zest

Pulp and juice of 2 limes
4½ cups sugar
Juice of 1 lemon

1. Cut the melon in half and remove the seeds. Using a sharp spoon or melon cutter, scrape out the pulp. You should have about 4 cups. Place in a large, heavy pot. Add the lime zest, lime pulp, and juice. Heat to boiling and stir in the sugar. Return to boiling and boil until a spoonful of jam thickens when placed on a chilled plate, about 45 minutes.

2. Add the lemon juice to the jam. Pour into sterilized jars and seal. Store in a cool place.

MAKES 3 PINTS

✻

FEAST OF ST. ANDREW —
NOVEMBER 30

ANDREW WAS THE BROTHER of Peter and was one of the twelve disciples. He was martyred on a cross shaped like the letter X around A.D. 60. It was Andrew, at the feeding of the five thousand, who spotted the lad with "five barley loaves and two small fishes" and asked ". . . what are they among so many?" He attended the Last Supper and witnessed the Ascension. It is generally recognized that Andrew went forth to preach the gospel, but his final resting place is a matter of conjecture. He was reportedly put to death at Patrae in Achaea (in present-day Greece). His bones were then either moved to Constantinople and on to Amalfi, or, as Scottish legend has it, taken to Scotland in the fourth century by St. Regulus. On the way, the ship crashed off the coast of Scotland near the present site of the town of St. Andrews. St. Andrew eventually became the patron saint of Scotland. In honor of Andrew, Scottish descendants around the world have created St. Andrew's Societies, organized to help the needy. Every year, the societies hold their annual dinners and exchange telegrams of good will and congratulations.

▪ ICED SCONES ▪

I have had the pleasure of visiting Scotland and found it a truly remarkable and beautiful country. One of the recipes I brought back with me was this one for wonderful iced scones.

2 cups all-purpose flour
½ teaspoon baking soda
½ teaspoon cream of tartar
½ teaspoon salt
2 tablespoons chilled unsalted butter
¾ to 1 cup buttermilk
Cornmeal

ICING
¼ cup confectioners' sugar
2 teaspoons milk
1½ teaspoons Scotch whiskey
½ teaspoon vanilla extract

1. Preheat oven to 475° F. Sift the flour with the baking soda, cream of tartar, and salt into a large bowl. Add the butter. Blend with a pastry blender until well incorporated. With a wooden spoon, stir in enough buttermilk, starting with ¾ cup, to form a soft dough.

2. Turn the dough out on a well-floured pastry board. Sprinkle lightly with flour. Knead for 2 minutes.

3. Divide the dough in half. Shape each half into a ball. Roll each ball out ½ inch thick. Cut each into four pie-shaped wedges.

4. Sprinkle a baking sheet with cornmeal. Place the scones on the sheet about 1 inch apart. Bake until golden brown, 15 to 20 minutes.

5. Combine the confectioners' sugar with the milk, whiskey, and vanilla. Drizzle over the hot scones. Serve while still warm.

MAKES 8 SCONES

WINTER RECIPES

Latkes

Gingerbread

Meatball Soup

Wassail

Hot Tea Toddy

Bizcochitos

Plymouth Succotash

Baked Lamb Stew

St. Lucia Chicken

Bruce Scott's Gravlax

Hoppin' John

Golden Skillet Cake

Pickled Smelts

Tangy Broiled Fish Steaks

Baked Pork Chops in Burgundy

Chicken Steamed with Ham and Vegetables

Spicy Groundhogs

Mardi Gras Filé Gumbo

Classic Breakfast Pancakes

Abraham Lincoln's Favorite Steak

Carrot-Nut Marmalade

Hubert's White Chocolate Mousse

Philadelphia Pepperpot

Date Shake

Red-Chile Stew

❋

WINTER

❊

I WAS BORN virtually on winter's doorstep—at 1:25 A.M. on December 23, for the record. I have always liked winter and in fact enjoy nothing more than taking the dog out for a romp in the snow that occasionally blankets New York's Riverside Park. I have mixed feelings, however, about being born so close to Christmas. One's birthday tends to get lost in the shuffle. There is always so much to be done: shopping for gifts, wrapping those gifts, making cookies and candy for stocking stuffers, planning Christmas Day dinner, doing the grocery shopping, preparing the dinner, cleaning house, and making sure all the dishes are clean. There isn't much time for a real birthday celebration. Even when friends go out of their way to remember, Christmas still hovers like a cloud waiting to burst. And burst it does, as it always did the day after my birthday, with the rituals of Christmas Eve.

As already noted, I grew up in a very religious household. Though we *all* attended my father's church regularly, the Christmas Eve service was the one church service that I truly enjoyed. Every year, the children of the congregation recited the Christmas story, as related in the Gospel of St. Luke:

And it came to pass in those days, that there went out a decree from Caesar Augustus, that all the world should be taxed. (And this taxing was first made when Cyrenius was governor of Syria.) And all went to be taxed, every one into his own city. And Joseph also went up from Galilee, out of the city of Nazareth, into Judea, unto the city of David, which is called Bethlehem; (because he was of the house and lineage of David:) To be taxed with Mary his espoused wife, being great with child. And so it was, that, while they were there, the days were accomplished that she should be delivered. And she brought forth her first born son and wrapped him in swaddling clothes, and laid him in a manger, because there was no room for them in the inn.

The children, tucked in next to the towering Christmas tree, were divided by age. Facing the congregation, each group stood as they told their part of the story. The kindergarten kids began the recitation and sometimes needed a guiding hand (my father's) to finish their part. The older children, not yet confirmed, concluded the recital. The narratives were interspersed with Christmas hymns. Some were sung by the children, some by the adult choir, and some by the whole congregation, the singing voices filling the church to the very tip of its steeple.

The arrival of the winter solstice on or about December 22, and the arrival of Christmas on the 25th, may not be entirely coincidental. It is believed by some that Christmas falls when it does because it was the church's only way to combat the pagan rites of gloom-chasing bonfires, illuminations, and celebrations of all kinds. Early Romans, for instance, paid tribute to the god Saturn with fires, while we string Christmas-tree lights on our houses and our Christmas trees.

■ DECEMBER ■

*We wish you Health, and good
Fires; Victuals, Drink and good
Stomachs, innocent Diversion,
and good Company; honest Trading,
and good success; loving Courtship
and good Wives, and lastly a merry
CHRISTMAS and a happy NEW
YEAR.*

—*VIRGINIA ALMANACK, 1766*

Despite the "ten" (*decem*) in its name, December is the twelfth month of the Gregorian calendar. When the early Roman calendar of ten months was changed to the twelve-month system we use today, December kept its slot as the final month of the year. (Though it lost it briefly when January and February were originally tacked on to the end of the calendar year.) Christian Saxons called December *Heligh-monath,* or "holy month," in deference to the birth of the Christ child.

✳

HANUKKAH — GENERALLY IN DECEMBER

HANUKKAH (OR CHANNUKAH) is the Hebrew "Feast of Dedication," which begins on the twenty-fifth day of Kislev, the third month of the Hebrew calendar, and lasts for eight days. It is a joyous holiday that can be traced back more than two thousand years to around 165 B.C. The Hebrews, under the control of the Syrian king, Antiochus Epiphanes, rebelled when he ordered that an altar to the Greek god Zeus be erected in the Temple in Jerusalem. Led by Judah Maccabee and his family, the Hebrews reclaimed Jerusalem from the Syrians after a fierce battle. Afterward, when the Hebrews returned to their desecrated Temple to relight the eternal flame and cleanse and rededicate the Temple, they found that only one vessel of holy oil was left undefiled—just enough to last for one day. Miraculously, the oil lasted eight days, until more oil could be brought to Jerusalem. Those eight days are reflected in the eight candles of the menorah. The lighting of the menorah is integral to the Hanukkah celebration. It is traditional to light the eight candles from left to right, one each day until the entire menorah is ablaze. The occasion is marked by singing, playing games, telling riddles, and exchanging presents.

Traditional Hanukkah dishes derive from legend and custom. Latkes (potato pancakes) have become symbolic of the observance. Originally consisting of just flour and water, latkes were made on the fly as the Hebrews prepared for battle. Today, the act of making latkes for Hanukkah symbolizes that battle, and the oil used for frying the pancakes represents the cleansing and rededication of the Temple.

▪ LATKES ▪

*F*or dinner one night when I was little, my mother made potato pancakes. I hated them—
so much, in fact, that I refused to eat. My father, taking no pity, made me sit at the
table until I ate them. I never did. I finally was sent to my room (slightly hungry, but relieved)
—and my mother never made them again. I can still recognize that sour, earthy taste of the
potatoes that I rejected as a kid, but I discovered by accident that if you grate the potatoes
twice, the pancakes have a sweeter, "cleaner" taste. The following recipe was passed on by
Myra Greene, who gave many great latke parties before her sudden death in 1985. Myra was
the sister of the late food writer Bert Greene and was one of the original founders of The Store
in Amagansett, one of the first gourmet takeout shops in America.

1½ pounds baking potatoes	2 tablespoons all-purpose flour
Juice of 1 lemon	2 teaspoons baking powder
1 small onion, finely grated	Salt and freshly ground pepper
1 large egg, lightly beaten	Vegetable shortening

1. Preheat the oven to 250° F. Peel the potatoes and roughly grate them into a
large bowl of cold water to which you have added the lemon juice. Let stand for
30 minutes.

2. Drain the potatoes and squeeze them dry with your hands. Place them in a
food processor. Process, using the pulse switch, until finely grated but not wet.
Transfer to a large bowl. Add the onion, egg, flour, baking powder, and salt and
pepper to taste. Stir until smooth.

3. Heat a large cast-iron skillet over medium heat until hot. Add enough vegetable shortening to coat the bottom of the pan lightly. Using a large tablespoon, spoon
the batter into the pan and let cook until brown and puffed, about 1 minute. Turn
over and brown the other sides. Place the cooked latkes on a rack over a cookie sheet
and keep warm in the oven until all the batter has been used.

SERVES 4

✳

FEAST OF ST. NICHOLAS — DECEMBER 6

NOT MUCH IS KNOWN about St. Nicholas other than that his real name was Bishop Myra, that he came from Lycia (in Asia Minor), and that he lived in the fourth century. There are several legends about the bishop, however. The most popular holds that he was a man who inherited great wealth and devoted it, and himself, to charity. He became the patron saint of children and gift giving and, of course, the model for the Dutch *Sinterklaas* and the German *Santa Klaus,* both derived from Sint Nikolaus, or Saint Nicholas.

In Dutch communities, there is almost always a parade to celebrate the arrival of St. Nick, who comes riding into town on his trusty white horse. His helper, *Zwarte Piet* (or "little black Pete"), walks at his side. It is said that *Zwarte Piet* is the one who actually climbs down the chimneys to deliver the presents and collect the gingerbread that people have left out. Or, if you have been naughty and not nice, Piet might leave raw onions and lumps of coal instead of presents in your wooden shoes. So beware.

■ GINGERBREAD ■

Gingerbread is wonderful any time of year, though there is something almost soul-satisfying about eating it slightly warm on a cold winter's day. Whipped cream is optional.

½ cup (1 stick) unsalted butter

1 cup sugar

2 eggs

1 cup buttermilk

2 teaspoons baking soda

1 cup molasses

2½ cups all-purpose flour

½ teaspoon ground cinnamon

½ teaspoon ground cloves

2 teaspoons ground ginger

½ cup dried currants

1. Preheat the oven to 375° F. Grease and flour a 9-inch square cake pan.

2. In a large bowl, beat the butter with the sugar until light and fluffy. Beat in the eggs, one at a time, beating well after each addition.

3. In another bowl, combine the buttermilk with the baking soda. Stir in the molasses.

4. In a medium bowl, combine the flour with the cinnamon, cloves, and ginger. Stir in the currants.

5. Add the flour mixture to the butter mixture in three parts, alternating with the molasses mixture. Mix well.

6. Pour the batter into the prepared pan. Bake until a toothpick inserted in the center comes out clean, 50 to 60 minutes. Cool before cutting into squares.

SERVES 6 TO 8

❊

✳

DAY OF OUR LADY OF GUADALUPE—DECEMBER 12

IN DECEMBER 1533, legend has it, an Indian, Juan Diego, saw the Virgin Mother on a hill near Mexico City. She instructed him to have the bishop build a shrine to her on that very site. The bishop refused to believe that Diego had actually seen the Virgin Mother. Three days later, at the same spot, the Virgin reappeared. She instructed Juan Diego to pick the roses suddenly growing out of the barren hillside and take them to the bishop as proof. When he got to the bishop, Diego opened his cloak and roses cascaded to the floor. An image of the Virgin Mary appeared on the cloak, making the bishop a believer. The shrine was built, and a piece of that cloak is preserved there to this day. The Lady of Guadalupe eventually gained status as the patron saint not only of Mexico City, but of the entire country. A feast day in her honor is also celebrated in the American Southwest, and one of the best places to witness and partake of this celebration is Tortugas, New Mexico.

As evening falls on December 10, drumbeats sound throughout this Indian village, signaling the beginning of the fiesta. Fourteen masked dancers dance the night away while the image of the Virgin Mother is carried to the Casa del Pueblo, the town hall, or meetinghouse. At 7:30 the next morning, pilgrims gather to march the four miles to the top of Tortugas Mountain. Mass is said at 11:00 A.M., and the faithful receive yucca stalks and blades of *sotol* root that serve as *quiotes* (staffs) for the trek back to town. That evening, the village comes alive with drums, songs, and dances. The morning of the 12th, the Day of Our Lady of Guadalupe, begins with another mass. The costumed dancers perform until noon, at which time the feasting begins as long tables are spread with spicy meatball soup, *frijoles,* fry bread, chile, and other Indian specialties. For more information, contact the Our Lady of Guadalupe Festival at (505) 526-8171.

▪ MEATBALL SOUP ▪

*T*his soup is native to the Southwest, and just about everyone has his or her own version.
The following is for a very simple soup that is generally served as a first course in shallow
soup bowls.

MEATBALLS
½ pound ground beef or veal
⅓ cup fine bread crumbs
1 small egg, lightly beaten
3 tablespoons milk
¼ teaspoon ground coriander
2 tablespoons finely chopped canned
   mild green chiles
¼ teaspoon salt
⅛ teaspoon freshly ground pepper
1 small shallot, minced

SOUP
4 cups chicken stock, thoroughly
   degreased
1 small carrot, cut into 2-inch strips
1 small zucchini, cut into 2-inch strips
1 small parsnip, cut into 2-inch pieces
3 to 4 tablespoons chopped fresh
   cilantro (to taste)

1. *To make the meatballs:* In a large bowl, combine the meat with the bread
crumbs, egg, and milk. Mix thoroughly and add the coriander, chiles, salt, pepper,
and shallot. Mix well and form into small (marble-size) meatballs.

2. *To make the soup:* Heat the stock to boiling; reduce the heat. Add the vegetables
and cook for 5 minutes. Add the meatballs and cook, skimming the surface frequently, for 10 minutes. Keep the soup at a simmer; do not allow it to boil. Stir in
the cilantro and serve in shallow soup bowls.

SERVES 4

❊

WASSAIL is a hot wine or ale punch that dates back to Saxon times, when it was traditional to go "wassailing" on New Year's Eve and Day, drinking and wishing everybody a merry old time. The term *wassail* is also a toast. It comes from the Middle English *wassayl,* a contraction of *waes hael* ("be whole"), which in turn is derived from the Old Norse *vesheill* ("be in good health").

The folks in Woodstock, Vermont, have moved the celebration to early December. This charming New England village is picture perfect, complete with village green and covered bridge. The Wassail Celebration is a three-day affair that begins with a fancy Friday-night ball. On Saturday the highlight of the day is the horse-and-carriage parade. Only horses and carriages are allowed, creating a charming atmosphere, particularly when the snow is falling. And, of course, the wassailing bowl is always full. For more information, contact the Woodstock area Chamber of Commerce at (802) 857-3555.

▪ WASSAIL ▪

*T*he following recipe gives my version of this seasonal drink.

½ cup sugar	3 cups dry red wine
2 cinnamon sticks	½ cup dry sherry
1 cup water	¼ cup lemon juice
1 cup pineapple juice	1 lemon, sliced
1 cup orange juice	

1. In a small saucepan, combine the sugar, cinnamon sticks, and water. Heat to boiling, reduce the heat, and simmer for 5 minutes. Let cool and discard the cinnamon sticks.

2. In a medium noncorrosive saucepan, combine the pineapple juice, orange juice, red wine, sherry, and lemon juice. Heat to just below boiling. Add the syrup and pour into a heatproof bowl. Garnish with lemon slices. Serve hot.

SERVES 8 TO 10

ON DECEMBER 16, 1773, a company of sixty men, dressed as Indians, stole aboard a British ship tied up in Boston Harbor and threw its cargo of tea overboard to protest import taxes levied by Great Britain. This event is recognized in American history as one of several confrontations with the British that led to rebellion and the Revolution. Every year since 1895, the Daughters of the American Revolution (DAR) have held a tea party to commemorate this event. It's a private affair for members, but a few select state and local government officials are invited as well. On the Sunday nearest December 16, the Boston Tea Party Ship and Museum stages a reenactment of the event. Tea and coffee are served. For more information on the reenactment, contact the Boston Tea Party Ship and Museum at (617) 338-1773.

■ HOT TEA TODDY ■

I suppose that there is something a bit ironic in drinking tea in any form in observance of the Boston Tea Party. But why not? Times have indeed changed.

1 teaspoon sugar	1 breakfast tea bag (or tea of choice)
3 whole cloves	3 ounces boiling water
1 cinnamon stick (about 1 inch long)	2 ounces hot bourbon
1 thin slice lemon	Freshly grated nutmeg

1. Place the sugar, cloves, cinnamon stick, lemon slice, and tea bag in a heavy mug. Add 1 ounce boiling water. Stir well and let stand for 5 minutes. Discard the tea bag.

2. Add the hot bourbon and the remaining 2 ounces boiling water to the mug. Stir. Sprinkle lightly with nutmeg.

SERVES 1

※

*LAS POSADAS—
DECEMBER 16-24*

IN THE SOUTHWEST, where the December air is scented by burning piñon branches, many celebrations are infused with spiritual overtones. The word *posada* means "lodging," and Las Posadas is an important Mexican (read Catholic) festival commemorating the journey of Mary and Joseph from Nazareth to Bethlehem and their search for shelter. Las Posadas processions are quite moving and beautiful to watch. In San Antonio, Texas, the missions hold candlelit processions, and mariachis play "Feliz Navidad" on the riverboats of the San Antonio River. In Santa Fe, New Mexico, worshipers carry small paper lanterns (*farolitos*) to light the way for "Mary and Joseph," who are refused shelter from store after store around the plaza while "the devil," who stands above on a balcony, calls them names. The devil is hissed at by the participants until, finally, everyone is allowed into the Palace of the Governors, where they are served hot cider and *bizcochitos* (aniseed cookies). Most major cities in the Southwest celebrate Las Posadas to some degree.

▪ BIZCOCHITOS ▪

These aniseed cookies are traditional for Christmas throughout the Southwest. There are a lot of different recipes for these cookies, but one thing they have in common is that they are made with lard. Vegetable shortening or a combination of shortening and butter may be substituted. The following recipe has been adapted from Huntley Dent's The Feast of Santa Fe *(Simon & Schuster, 1985), which is one of my all-time favorite cookbooks.*

½ cup lard or vegetable shortening (or
   half butter, half shortening)
⅔ cup sugar
1 egg
1 teaspoon aniseed
1 tablespoon brandy

1½ cups all-purpose flour
1 teaspoon baking powder
¼ teaspoon salt
¼ cup sugar mixed with ¼ teaspoon
   ground cinnamon

1. Preheat the oven to 350° F. Beat the shortening with the sugar until light. Beat in the egg, aniseed, and brandy.

2. In a medium bowl, combine the flour with the baking powder and salt. Stir into the shortening mixture with a wooden spoon until the mixture starts to form a mass. Gently knead into a soft dough. Refrigerate, covered, for 15 minutes.

3. Roll out the dough on a floured board about ¼ inch thick and cut out 2½-inch rounds (or any fancy shape). Dip one side into the sugar-cinnamon mixture and arrange on cookie sheets, sugar side up. Bake until the edges turn golden brown, about 12 minutes. Cool on a rack.

MAKES ABOUT 2 DOZEN

❋

I mused upon the Pilgrim flock
Whose luck it was to land
Upon almost the only rock
Among the Plymouth sand.

—ALDEN C. SPOONER,
OLD TIMES AND NEW

WHEN SPOONER wrote these lines for the New England Society Festival in 1896, he may have unwittingly sown the seeds of doubt as to where the Pilgrim fathers actually landed. Many historians say the *Mayflower* most likely touched ground on Cape Cod, on December 21, 1620 (according to the Gregorian calendar; it was December 11 on the Julian calendar then in use). And the famous rock? Well, as has been recorded, the story of Plymouth Rock was perpetuated by one Ruling Elder Thomas Faunce (in 1741!) who declared it to be the landing spot of the Pilgrims. Descendants of the Pilgrims instituted a holiday, Forefathers' Day, in 1769 to commemorate the landing and to keep the story alive. There was food aplenty at this celebration, set out on long communal tables: turkey, pigeon, venison, lobster, shellfish, succotash, johnny cake, Indian pudding, cranberry tarts—and a goodly supply of wine and rum to wash it all down.

An attempt, in 1774, to move the rather large boulder to the center of town for security reasons ended in disaster. The rock split in half. One half made it to the town square; the other stayed put. After decades of melodrama, the two pieces were reunited in 1880 and imbedded back in the sand. The only problem was that the chosen resting place was so far up the beach that celebrants, who made the sojourn to Plymouth for Forefathers' Day, began to wonder just how the *Mayflower* could have landed that far above the tide line. This went on until 1920, when it was decided to move the rock further down the beach. This time both halves split asunder. The result now sits, in the words of writer Perry Garfinkel, "like a caged animal in a granite portico at the edge of Plymouth Harbor."

The importance of Forefathers' Day, once a major event throughout the country, diminished in the late 1800s as Thanksgiving became the holiday synonymous with the Pilgrims. Then too, the post–Civil War era saw the rise of Christmas as a major commercial holiday.

▪ PLYMOUTH SUCCOTASH ▪

*P*lymouth Succotash is basically a thick bean puree with chunks of corned beef, poultry, and hominy. Nobody seems quite sure how this version of the classic corn-and-bean dish originated, but it certainly seems like a Yankee twist on a classic native dish. It takes a while to prepare, but it's wonderful on a cold winter's day.

1 cup dried white beans (pea or navy)
1 large onion, chopped
¼ teaspoon ground cloves
¼ teaspoon freshly ground pepper
1 corned beef brisket (2½ to 3 pounds)
1 chicken (about 3 pounds)
1 large onion stuck with 4 cloves
2 carrots, roughly chopped
1 parsnip, roughly chopped

1 stalk celery with leaves, broken
4 sprigs parsley
12 black peppercorns
1 small rutabaga (¾ to 1 pound), cut into ½-inch cubes
1 can (1 pound, 4 ounces) hominy
Salt and freshly ground pepper
3 tablespoons chopped fresh parsley

1. Soak the beans in cold water overnight (or boil for 2 minutes and let stand, covered, for 1 hour). Drain and place in a large pot with the chopped onion, ground cloves, and pepper. Cover with cold water and heat to boiling; reduce the heat. Simmer the beans, adding water if needed, until they are soft enough to mash, about 1 hour. Drain, reserving the liquid. Puree the beans in a food processor, adding only enough liquid as needed to process. Set aside.

2. Meanwhile, wash the brisket and trim it of fat. Place it in a large pot with the chicken, and add water to cover. Add the onion stuck with cloves, carrots, parsnip, celery, parsley, and peppercorns. Heat to boiling, reduce the heat, and cook, covered, until the chicken is tender, about 1 hour. Transfer the chicken to a plate. Cover and cool. Continue to cook the corned beef, covered, until tender, about 1½ hours longer. Transfer to a plate and cool. Strain the broth and measure off 6 cups. Add more water (or canned broth) if needed.

3. Place the 6 cups of broth in a large saucepan. Add the rutabaga and hominy; heat to boiling and reduce the heat. Simmer, covered, for 30 minutes.

4. Meanwhile, remove the chicken meat and cut it into 1-inch pieces. Discard the skin and bones. Cut the corned beef into 1-inch pieces and add to the chicken.

5. Add the pureed beans to the turnip-and-hominy mixture. Stir until smooth. Continue to cook for 15 minutes. Add the chicken and corned beef. Cook 15 minutes longer; the mixture should be thick. Add salt and pepper to taste. Sprinkle with parsley before serving.

SERVES 6

WINTER SOLSTICE—ON OR ABOUT DECEMBER 22

The winter solstice occurs about December 22, when the sun is at the southernmost point of its elliptic orbit. From this point until the vernal equinox in the Northern Hemisphere, the nights begin to shorten until, with the arrival of spring (about March 22), night and day are once again of equal length all over the earth.

✳

THE ACTUAL BIRTH date of Jesus Christ is not known. Dates as disparate as May 20, April 19, January 6, and December 25 have all been suggested by scholars. December 25, however, was chosen by the Western church, possibly because it coincided with pagan solstice rites. The traditions of the Yule log, mistletoe, the holly and ivy, the holiday tree, wassailing, and gift giving all stem from those rites.

Christmas is the most important Christian observance and is the only religious holiday that is also a federal holiday. It has become such a commercial venture that it is hard to believe that before the Civil War, the holiday was celebrated very quietly in religious circles only. It was not until after the war that retailers got savvy and turned the holiday into a shopper's dilemma. Nowadays, retailers can barely wait (and often don't) for Thanksgiving to be over before promoting Christmas—a far cry from New England's first Christmas.

The first New England Christmas was anything but festive. The Puritans did not believe in celebrating the birth of Christ. For many years, that point of view was forced on the others, or "strangers" as non-Puritans were labeled. By 1659 the Puritans had gone so far as to legally decree that "anybody who is found observing, by abstinence from labor, feasting, or any other way, any such days as Christmas Day, shall pay for every such offense five shillings."

Christmas was an important event in the household of my childhood. After the Christmas-morning service, my family gathered together for an early-afternoon Christmas dinner. We had a big family, and when the Schulzes got together, meals were somewhat rowdy affairs. The teasing and joking came dangerously close to getting out of hand on occasion, but for the most part, laughter prevailed.

I rarely get home for the holidays anymore, but I keep my own traditions alive by making Christmas dinner and surrounding myself with close friends. Christmas is a happy time. Even for those of us who have experienced the horrible pain of loss. Our perceptions of the holiday are forever altered, but the true meaning of Christmas and the joy of giving and receiving, and being with people we choose to be with, gets us through.

▪ BAKED LAMB STEW ▪

*A*s noted, I grew up in Colorado, one of our major lamb-producing states, but I never tasted lamb until I moved East. Now I eat it often. This stew—redolent of tomatoes, cognac, and orange—makes a wonderful Christmas dinner.

4 pounds boneless lamb (from the leg), cut into 1½-inch cubes
Salt and freshly ground pepper
½ cup all-purpose flour
¼ cup vegetable oil
2 large onions, chopped
2 large cloves garlic, minced
Pinch saffron
½ cup dry white wine

5 tomatoes peeled, chopped, and seeded (about 3½ pounds)
1 cup chicken stock or broth
1 tablespoon sugar
1 tablespoon unsalted butter
1 tablespoon finely slivered orange peel
¼ cup cognac, heated
Chopped fresh parsley

1. Preheat the oven to 375° F. Pat the lamb cubes dry, sprinkle them with salt and pepper, and dust with the flour.

2. In a large heavy pot or Dutch oven, heat the oil over medium heat. Brown the meat, a few pieces at a time, until very dark. Transfer to a plate.

3. Pour off all but 2 tablespoons of fat from the pot and add the onion and garlic. Cook, scraping the bottom and sides of pot, until golden, about 5 minutes. Sprinkle with saffron and stir in the wine, tomatoes, and stock. Sprinkle with sugar and heat to boiling. Cover and bake in the oven until the meat is tender, about 1 hour.

4. Melt the butter in a small saucepan. Add the orange peel and stir to coat. Add the cognac and carefully set aflame. When the flame subsides, add to the stew and return to the oven for another 20 minutes. (If the stew seems too thin, remove the cover during the last 20 minutes.) Sprinkle with parsley.

SERVES 6 TO 8

❋

KWANZAA—
DECEMBER 26 TO JANUARY 1

KWANZAA is a week-long cultural celebration observed by many African-Americans. The holiday was created in 1966 by Maulana Karenga, professor, author, and leading theorist of the Black Movement. The holiday is American, but it draws from the African harvest celebration. The word *kwanzaa* means "the first fruits of the harvest" in Kiswahili. In *Kwanzaa* (Gumbs & Thomas, New York, 1990), Cedric McClester explains that Kiswahili is a nontribal African language that is used in a large portion of the African continent. The seven principles (*Nguzo Saba*) of Kwanzaa were established to encourage black unity. During Kwanzaa, celebrants fast from sunrise to sunset to cleanse their bodies, souls, and minds. After sunset on each evening, one of seven candles is lit before the fast is broken. A black candle represents the people, three red candles signify the struggle, and three green candles symbolize the hopes and aspirations for the future. On December 31 the Kwanzaa *karamu* (feast) is observed. It is a time for sharing and rejoicing.

Kwanzaa menus reflect the African-American heritage, but there are no set dishes or rigid rules that have to be followed. Unofficially, most celebrants try to include meals or dishes from different countries in Africa, the Caribbean, and the southern United States—or, for that matter, from anywhere that might be called the African diaspora.

■ ST. LUCIA CHICKEN ■

On the lovely island of St. Lucia, near Grenada, caramel flavors many of the native chicken dishes. The following recipe is a good example of a regional dish that can be used for Kwanzaa.

1 chicken, cut into serving pieces
1 large clove garlic, bruised
3 tablespoons sugar
1/3 cup water
1 stalk celery
1 carrot, chopped
1 onion, chopped
1 tablespoon chopped fresh parsley

1 sprig fresh thyme, minced
1/4 teaspoon ground cumin
1/4 teaspoon crushed coriander seeds
1/4 teaspoon ground turmeric
1/4 teaspoon curry powder
Salt and freshly ground pepper
Chopped fresh parsley

1. Rub the chicken pieces with the bruised garlic. Mince the garlic and reserve.

2. Place the sugar in a large heavy pot or Dutch oven. Cook over medium-high heat until the sugar melts and turns deep brown. Reduce the heat to medium-low and stir in the water. Stir until all the sugar particles have dissolved. Add the chicken, skin side down, to the pot in one layer. Add the remaining ingredients through curry powder. Cook, covered, for 15 minutes. Turn the chicken over; cook, covered, 15 minutes longer.

3. When the chicken is done, transfer it to a serving dish and keep warm. Boil the contents of the pot until slightly thickened, about 5 minutes. Add salt and pepper to taste. Pour over the chicken and sprinkle with parsley.

SERVES 4

NEW YEAR'S EVE/FIRST NIGHT—DECEMBER 31

THIS NEW YEAR'S EVE, you might wish to take a walk in the deep woods to see for yourself if the animals really do kneel at midnight and the mighty rivers really do stop flowing, as is chronicled in American folklore. If the night is clear, look up. You might even see the moon stand still. But look quickly—you only have a few seconds. Yes, it's time to "let out the old, let in the new."

In days past, "letting in the new" referred to the custom of throwing open all the doors in one's house on New Year's Eve. As the fresh ("new") air swept in, the stale ("old") swept out. On the other hand, you may prefer to "ring out the old and ring in the new." This observance was originated by churches to mark the end of late-night prayer services and the beginning of the new year. The pealing of church bells seems a bit tame, however, when you consider that the pioneers celebrated the occasion by shooting their guns in the air. Today we simply make do with noisemak-ers, car horns, foghorns, and fireworks.

First Night celebrations originated in Boston in 1976 and are now observed in towns and cities all over the United States and Canada. First Night is actually a trademarked name, which is leased through the nonprofit International Alliance of First Night Celebrations. For a fee, a city gets to use the name and in return, receives information and staff support. The purpose of First Night celebrations is to provide the public, including children and the elderly, with entertainment and arts events that are family-oriented and alcohol-free. For information on obtaining First Night rights, contact First Night at (617) 542-1399. For local events, check your newspa-per.

■ BRUCE SCOTT'S GRAVLAX ■

My first New Year's Eve in New York was spent in Times Square waiting for the ball to drop. It was (and I guess still is) quite an amazing experience. Usually, however, I like to stay at home and watch it all on television. New Year's, of course, is a great night to have a small dinner party. And what better way to start the meal than with this incredible gravlax, which is the inspiration of my good friend Bruce Scott. It is difficult to make if you use less than 2 pounds of fish, but it keeps remarkably well.

1 fresh salmon fillet (about 2 pounds)
  skin on, all bones removed
2 tablespoons olive oil
1 tablespoon sugar
1½ teaspoons salt

½ teaspoon crushed white pepper
½ cup finely chopped fresh dill
3 tablespoons dry white wine
Mustard Sauce (recipe follows)

1. Brush the fish on both sides with olive oil. Combine the sugar, salt, pepper, and 1 tablespoon dill. Rub into the fish on both sides.

2. Sprinkle half the remaining dill over the bottom of a shallow glass or ceramic dish that will hold the fish snugly. Place the fish over the dill. Sprinkle the fish with wine and then with the remaining dill. Cover loosely with plastic wrap and place a heavy weight on top, making sure edges are sealed to sides of dish. Refrigerate for 48 hours, turning several times.

3. Meanwhile, make the Mustard Sauce.

4. *To serve:* Carefully remove the skin from the fish. Cut the fish on an angle into slices no more than ¼ inch thick. Serve with Mustard Sauce.

SERVES 8 TO 10 AS AN APPETIZER

MUSTARD SAUCE

1 tablespoon sugar
2 tablespoons Dijon mustard
3 tablespoons white-wine vinegar
¾ cup olive oil

1 teaspoon lemon juice
1 teaspoon chopped fresh dill
Salt and freshly ground pepper

In a small bowl, combine the sugar, mustard, and vinegar. Slowly whisk in the oil, 1 tablespoon at a time, until the mixture is thick. Whisk in the lemon juice and dill. Add salt and pepper to taste.

MAKES ABOUT 1 CUP

■ JANUARY ■

We looked upon a world unknown,
On nothing we could call our own.
Around the glistening wonder bent
The blue walls of the firmament,
No cloud above, no earth below, —
A universe of sky and snow!

—JOHN GREENLEAF WHITTIER,
"SNOWBOUND"

In the year 46 B.C., or thereabouts, January 1, the date on which elected Roman officials took office, became the "official" beginning of the new year. Up until this time, March had always marked the beginning of the year. The name "January" is derived from *Janus,* the god of gates and doors, or in a sense, of all beginnings.

❋

■ JANUARY SPECIAL EVENTS ■

NATIONAL FIBER FOCUS MONTH: Sponsored by General Mills to promote fiber as a healthy addition to the national diet.

NATIONAL OATMEAL MONTH: Sponsored by Quaker Oats to celebrate the mighty oat, particularly in the form of breakfast cereal.

NATIONAL PRUNE BREAKFAST MONTH: Sponsored by the California Prune Board in San Francisco to promote the beneficial properties of the prune, which are many.

NATIONAL SOUP MONTH: Sponsored by Campbell Soup, to celebrate the goodness of nutritious soup.

NATIONAL PIZZA WEEK — THIRD WEEK: Brought to us by Pizza Hut, to celebrate the fact that the average American eats seven whole pizzas per year.

✳

NEW YEAR'S DAY

JANUARY 1 is the first day of the first month of the Gregorian calendar year. It is a time to take stock and make resolutions. It is also the time not to take any chances with the year to come. So be wary what you eat on this first day of the year. Hoppin' John, a southern casserole of rice and black-eyed peas, is probably one of the best-known New Year's "good luck" foods in this country. Eating some will assure you of prosperity in the New Year—or so they say. Actually, many cultures believe that beans (which include black-eyed peas) represent hard work and diligence. There are other good-luck foods, as well. Pork with sauerkraut is a favorite in Ohio, the eating of which ensures that the devourers will not have to "scratch" for a living during the year ahead (steers paw the ground, chickens scratch). In the Northwest and other areas influenced by Scandinavians, cabbage is eaten because it is green, the color of money. In some places, herring and sardines are eaten because they travel in *abundant* numbers, and fish in general are considered lucky, because as everyone knows, fish always go forward.

▪ HOPPIN' JOHN ▪

To assure you and your family of a prosperous and happy year, be sure to fix this dish for lunch and dinner. It is excellent with roast fowl.

1 package (10 ounces) frozen black-eyed
  peas
2 strips bacon
1 small onion, chopped
1 clove garlic, minced
1 cup cooked rice

2 tablespoons red-wine vinegar
Salt and freshly ground pepper
¼ cup finely chopped fresh chives or
  scallion (white parts only)
2 tablespoons chopped fresh parsley

1. Drop the frozen peas into boiling salted water in a medium saucepan. Simmer until tender, about 20 minutes. Drain, reserving ¼ cup cooking liquid.

2. In a large, heavy skillet over medium heat, sauté the bacon strips until crisp. Drain on paper toweling. Reserve.

3. Stir the onion into the bacon drippings in the skillet. Cook for 3 minutes. Add the garlic; cook for 2 minutes. Stir in the drained peas and the rice. Cook, stirring constantly, until warmed through. Add the vinegar and enough reserved cooking liquid from the peas to moisten the mixture (2 to 3 tablespoons). Cook for 5 minutes.

4. Season to taste with salt and pepper. Crumble the reserved bacon over the top. Sprinkle with chives and parsley.

SERVES 4 TO 6

❋

MARTIN LUTHER KING, JR.'S BIRTHDAY — THIRD WEEKEND IN JANUARY

MARTIN LUTHER KING, JR., the black civil-rights leader who was assassinated in 1968, was born on January 15, 1929, in Atlanta, Georgia. His birthday is a national holiday celebrated on the third Monday of January. The son of a Baptist minister, King himself was ordained at the age of nineteen. After graduating from Morehouse College, he continued his divinity studies at Crozer Theological Seminary in Chester, Pennsylvania. King was a remarkable man. He was influenced by Mahatma Gandhi and, in fact, went to India in 1959 to study Gandhi's techniques of nonviolence. He led many civil-rights marches and demonstrations around the South and organized voter registration drives. King was awarded the Nobel Peace Prize in 1964. He was also spit at, stoned, jailed, stabbed, and eventually assassinated, all because he stood up for civil rights and fought for jobs, fair housing, and voting rights for the poor, both black and white.

■ GOLDEN SKILLET CAKE ■

It has become somewhat of a tradition to celebrate Martin Luther King Day with a Southern-style breakfast. This old-fashioned skillet cake is somewhat like Yorkshire pudding but baked in a cast-iron skillet until puffed and golden. It can be served with a fruit topping, or with maple syrup and a side of sausage or ham.

¼ cup (½ stick) unsalted butter

3 eggs

¾ cup milk

2 tablespoons fresh orange juice

¾ cup all-purpose flour

Pinch freshly grated nutmeg

Confectioners' sugar

1. Preheat the oven to 425° F.

2. Place the butter in a heavy 2-quart skillet or pan no more than 3 inches deep. Place in oven until butter melts.

3. Meanwhile, beat the eggs in a large bowl until light. Beat in the milk, orange juice, flour, and nutmeg until smooth.

4. Swirl the melted butter around bottom and sides of skillet. Pour in the batter and return to the oven. Bake 25 minutes, or until golden brown and puffed up. Dust with confectioners' sugar and serve immediately.

SERVES 2 TO 4

✳

CASTLE ROCK SMELT DERBY—SOMETIME BETWEEN JANUARY AND MARCH

THE ANNUAL SMELT RUN up Washington's Cowlitz River can occur any-time during January, February, or March. It's all up to the fish. So if you're planning on going "smelt dipping," you have to be flexible. Once the run is under way, however, it lasts only about two weeks. The river is so teeming with fish that the participants in the derby merely have to stand on the riverbank and dip nets in the water to catch the smelts. It doesn't sound very sporting, but it's not as easy as it sounds. The limit is twenty per day. You can have your catch cleaned and fried on the spot, tables are set up on the riverbank for dining, and beer on tap is available for the thirsty. You can also get your catch pickled and take it home with you. For more information, contact the Castle Rock Chamber of Commerce at (206) 274-6603.

■ PICKLED SMELTS ■

Smelts are often fried—bones and all if the fish are small enough—and eaten whole. Another popular way to prepare the fish, particularly when they are larger, is to pickle them in the Eastern European tradition.

2 quarts smelts (or sardines or anchovies), cleaned, heads removed	2 teaspoons pickling spices
	2 small bay leaves
½ cup coarse or pickling salt	¾ cup sugar
2 onions, sliced	2 cups white vinegar

1. Sprinkle the smelts with the salt. Let them stand for 10 hours. Rinse the fish six times in cold water and drain. Cut into pieces.

2. Place the fish in two sterilized 1-quart jars. Add 1 sliced onion, 1 teaspoon pickling spices, and 1 small bay leaf to each jar.

3. In a small saucepan, combine the sugar and vinegar. Heat to boiling, reduce the heat, and simmer, uncovered, for 5 minutes. Pour over the fish. Cover and let cool. Refrigerate for at least 3 days before serving. Store in the refrigerator.

MAKES 2 QUARTS

❋

※

CHINESE NEW YEAR — BETWEEN JANUARY 21 AND FEBRUARY 19

THE CHINESE NEW YEAR begins at sunset on the day of the second new moon following the winter solstice—or the day of the first full moon after the sun enters the sign of Aquarius (sometime between January 20 and February 19). The complex Chinese calendar is based on a system that goes as far back as the twenty-seventh century B.C.! Each year is named for one of twelve animals, which were originally selected on the basis of a cross-country race of all kinds of creatures. According to legend, the winners, in the following order, were the rat, ox, tiger, hare, dragon, serpent, horse, ram, monkey, rooster, dog, and boar. There are five elements associated with the New Year, as well: fire, earth, wood, water, and metal.

Chinese New Year celebrations are popular events wherever there is a sizable Chinese population. The dragon parades, featuring oversized puppets, floats, and firecrackers blasting the night air, are always fun to watch and inevitably attract a crowd. The centerpiece of all these parades is the Golden Dragon. Made of silk and velvet, it can be up to twenty-five feet long, and is propped up by sticks, supported by the young men who provide the legs for the colorful beast.

In Chinese homes, eating fish on New Year's Day is considered a good omen. *Yu* is the word for "fish" in Chinese. Its homonym means "abundance" or "surplus." Hence, eating fish will ensure an abundance of blessings in the coming year.

▪ TANGY BROILED FISH STEAKS ▪

The marinade given below is delicious on any fish steak: swordfish, tuna, bluefish, and even salmon. It is also good on monkfish and cod or any fish that can be thickly filleted.

4 fish steaks (about 1 inch thick)
½ cup soy sauce
¼ cup dry sherry
1 tablespoon sesame seeds
1 tablespoon sesame oil

1½ teaspoons minced fresh ginger
1 clove garlic, minced
4 scallions, chopped
½ teaspoon grated lemon peel

1. Place the fish in a glass or ceramic dish. Combine the remaining ingredients and pour over the fish. Marinate, covered and refrigerated, turning once, for 1 hour.

2. Preheat the broiler.

3. Place the fish on a broiler tray and broil very near the heat for 4 to 5 minutes per side.

SERVES 4

✳

ST. VINCENT'S FEAST DAY —
JANUARY 22

ST. VINCENT was a Spanish deacon who was martyred in A.D. 304. At the time, Christianity was banned in Saragossa, Spain, where he lived. He was captured and, after refusing to denounce his beliefs, brutally tortured. It's said that on one occasion, his jailer witnessed a bright white light coming into Vincent's darkened cell. The jailer converted on the spot—and the white light turned Vincent's pain to ecstasy. His captors eventually gave up, aware that Vincent would never denounce his God. At that point, Vincent died from his injuries. It is not known how he became the patron saint of wine growers, but it might have started in Burgundy, France, where he was always held in high regard. It is said that if the sun shines on January 22, the wine growers will have a great year.

▪ BAKED PORK CHOPS IN BURGUNDY ▪

This recipe is easy to prepare and absolutely delicious. It goes well with rice or potatoes.

4 thick pork chops
Salt and freshly ground pepper
½ cup all-purpose flour
2 tablespoons vegetable oil
1 tablespoon unsalted butter

1 small white onion, finely chopped
1 clove garlic, minced
½ cup sliced mushroom caps
1 cup red Burgundy
Chopped fresh parsley

1. Preheat the oven to 350° F.

2. Trim all fat from the pork chops. Sprinkle each well with salt and pepper. Rub the seasonings into the meat and dredge with flour, shaking off excess.

3. Heat the oil and butter in a large heavy skillet over medium heat. Sauté the chops until golden brown and crisp, about 5 minutes per side. Transfer to a baking dish.

4. Add the onion to the skillet; cook over medium-low heat for 1 minute. Add the garlic; cook for 3 minutes. Raise the heat to medium-high and add the mushrooms. Cook, stirring constantly, until the mushrooms begin to brown, 4 to 5 minutes. Add the wine and continue to cook over high heat until reduced by half. Pour the sauce over the meat.

5. Bake in the oven, basting several times, for 40 minutes, or until the meat juices run clear when the meat is pricked with a fork. Sprinkle with parsley.

SERVES 4

*

TET NGUYEN DAN, meaning the Feast of the First Day (the first day of the lunar new year), is the most important holiday of the Vietnamese, who have settled in large numbers in this country. In San Jose, they have been celebrating "Tet" for about ten years now, and the festival is a colorful affair. Centuries-old traditions are observed, along with arts, crafts, and sporting events. The food, of course, is Vietnamese, and there is a remarkable variety to be sampled. More than forty restaurants participate in this event. For more information, contact the Tet Festival at (408) 295-9210.

■ CHICKEN STEAMED WITH HAM ■ AND VEGETABLES

One of the reasons Vietnamese dishes are so popular in this country is that most of them are light-tasting and low in fat, and are fairly quick and easy to prepare. The following steamed dish is quite unusual. Everything is steamed together, making one tidy package.

5 chicken thighs, skinned, boned, cut into 1-inch-wide strips
1 small onion, finely chopped
1 clove garlic, minced
2 shallots, finely chopped
3 teaspoons *nuoc mam*
3/4 teaspoon salt
1/4 teaspoon freshly ground pepper

1 1/2 teaspoons sugar
5 slices boiled ham
2 stalks bok choy (Chinese cabbage), or 1/2 pound regular cabbage, or 1 pound string beans
2 teaspoons cornstarch
1/2 teaspoon soy sauce
1 cup chicken stock

1. In a medium bowl, combine the chicken strips, onion, garlic, shallot, 1 teaspoon *nuoc mam*, ½ teaspoon salt, the pepper, and ½ teaspoon sugar. Mix well.

2. Cut each slice of ham into four pieces. Arrange them, overlapping, over the bottom and sides of a lightly buttered 3-cup bowl. Place the chicken mixture in the center; pat down to firm.

3. Set the bowl in a wok or pan. Add enough boiling water to reach halfway up the sides. Cover and steam the chicken for 40 minutes in all. If you are using bok choy, cut it into 2-inch pieces; slice each piece in half. Place the bok choy over the chicken after 35 minutes and steam 5 minutes longer. If you use regular cabbage, cut it into wedges. Place the cabbage over the chicken after 28 minutes and steam 12 minutes longer. If you are using string beans, slice them in the French manner, trimming the ends and slicing them in half lengthwise. Place them over the chicken after 30 minutes and steam 10 minutes longer.

4. Meanwhile, prepare the sauce: Combine the cornstarch, 2 teaspoons *nuoc mam*, ¼ teaspoon salt, 1 teaspoon sugar, soy sauce, and stock. Heat to boiling, lower the heat, and simmer until thick, about 20 minutes.

5. When the chicken and vegetables are tender, uncover and place the vegetables on a platter. Spoon the chicken over the vegetables, and then spoon the sauce over the top. Serve with rice.

SERVES 4

NOTE: *Nuoc mam* is a pungent fish sauce available in most Asian markets.

February—February—
How your moods of action vary
Or to seek or shun;
Now a smile of sunlight lifting
Now in chilly snowflakes drifting;
Now with icy shuttles reaping
Silvery webs are spun.
Now with bells you blithely sing
'Neath the stars or sun;
Now a blade of burdock bring
To the suff'ring one;
February you are very
Dear, when all is done;
May blessings rest above you
You, who one day
(and so we love you)
Gave us Washington.

—WILL CARLETON

The second month of the Gregorian calendar, February derives from the Latin *Februarius,* which itself derives from *februa,* or "rites of purification." These rites were celebrated in early Roman days, when February was, for a while, the *last* month of the year, with March heralding in the new.

❋

■ FEBRUARY SPECIAL EVENTS ■

CANNED FOOD MONTH: Sponsored by the Canned Food Information Council to promote the convenience and practicality of canned foods.

GREAT AMERICAN PIES MONTH: Sponsored by Eagle Brand Sweetened Condensed Milk to encourage the return to the pleasures of baking.

NATIONAL CHERRY MONTH: Sponsored by the National Red Cherry Institute Riverview Center to promote the sour cherry and its many uses.

NATIONAL GRAPEFRUIT MONTH: Proclaimed by Congress, according to the Florida Department of Citrus, the sponsor of this month-long celebration of the grapefruit.

NATIONAL KRAUT AND FRANKFURTER WEEK—THE WEEK CONTAINING FEBRUARY 14: Sponsored by the National Kraut Packers' Association to celebrate one of America's favorite combinations: sauerkraut and hot dogs.

FHA/HERO WEEK—THE SECOND FULL WEEK: Sponsored by the Future Homemakers of America. (HERO stands for Home Economics Related Occupation.)

❋

✳

GROUNDHOG DAY —
FEBRUARY 2

THE MOST FAMOUS groundhog of all time, without a doubt, lives in Punxsu-tawney, Pennsylvania, about ninety miles north of Pittsburgh. Every year on Febru-ary 2, the eyes of the country turn toward Punxsutawney, where that groundhog, named Phil, predicts the weather ahead. If he sees his own shadow, of course, don't put those winter coats away just yet.

The Germans brought the tradition of Groundhog Day to Pennsylvania from Europe, where the hedgehog reigned supreme. However, agricultural societies around the world have long considered February 2 as the day for predicting the weather ahead. The secular observance also coincides with the religious holiday of Candlemas, which celebrates the purification of the Blessed Virgin Mary and is highlighted by the procession of candle-bearing believers. An old rhyme has it:

If Candlemas Day be fair and clear,
There'll be five winters in the year.

■ SPICY GROUNDHOGS ■

Writer Elaine Light of Punxsutawney immortalized the groundhog in a delightful cook-book, The New Gourmets and Groundhogs, *the proceeds of which go to charity. Her recipe for groundhog cookies follows. The book (and special groundhog cookie cutter) can be ordered from the Easter Seal Society of Punxsutawney, Punxsutawney, PA 15767.*

2 cups sifted all-purpose flour
½ teaspoon salt
½ teaspoon baking soda
1 teaspoon baking powder
1 teaspoon ground ginger
1 teaspoon ground cloves
1½ teaspoons ground cinnamon

½ cup (1 stick) unsalted butter, softened
1 cup sugar
½ cup molasses
1 egg yolk
1 egg, lightly beaten
Currants or raisins

1. Sift the flour with the salt, baking soda, baking powder, ginger, cloves, and cinnamon into a bowl.

2. In a large bowl, beat the butter with the sugar until light and fluffy. Beat in the molasses and egg yolk. Slowly stir in the flour mixture and mix well. Form into a ball and refrigerate, covered, for 1 hour.

3. Preheat the oven to 350° F. Divide the dough into three batches. Roll out the dough, one batch at a time, on a sugar-sprinkled board, ⅛ inch thick. Cut the cookies out with a floured groundhog cookie cutter. Place the cookies on greased baking sheets and brush lightly with beaten egg. Add a currant or raisin for the eye. Bake for 8 to 10 minutes, or until edges are crisped. Cool slightly before removing from the baking sheet.

MAKES 12 TO 15 LARGE,
OR 3 ½ TO 4 DOZEN SMALL, GROUNDHOGS

MARDI GRAS —
TUESDAY BEFORE ASH WEDNESDAY

MARDI GRAS, "fat Tuesday" in French, is the last day of the carnival season, which in New Orleans opens officially on Epiphany with the Twelfth Night Revelers' Ball. Though Mardi Gras is celebrated in many U.S. cities, including Biloxi, Mississippi, and Mobile, Alabama, the event is synonymous with New Orleans, where it was introduced about 1830. (Some say that it may have been celebrated as early as 1699 by French colonists camped on the riverbanks where New Orleans now stands.) It was not until 1857, however, that the first parade was held by a secret society called the Mistick Krewe of Comus. Today there are more than sixty groups (krewes) involved. On Mardi Gras, New Orleans is a riot of colors and merriment. The festivities include parades, balls, parties, and more parties. For more information on visiting New Orleans for Mardi Gras, contact the Greater New Orleans Tourist and Convention Commission at (504) 566-5011.

▪ MARDI GRAS FILÉ GUMBO ▪

*I*n 1979 I had the good fortune to travel on assignment with the late Bert Greene to New Orleans and Louisiana's Cajun country. We racked up quite a few gumbos. This is just one of them.

¼ cup vegetable oil
¼ cup all-purpose flour
2 large onions, chopped
5 tablespoons unsalted butter
4 cups coarsely chopped fresh okra
2⅔ cups chopped, seeded tomatoes
2 large green bell peppers, seeded and
   chopped
4 cloves garlic, minced
2½ pounds shrimps, shelled and
   deveined
1½ quarts chicken stock

2 cups water
2 tablespoons hot red pepper flakes
Salt
2 bay leaves, crumbled
2 teaspoons Worcestershire sauce
1 teaspoon ground allspice
¼ teaspoon dried thyme
Freshly ground pepper
Steamed rice
Filé powder (see Note)
Hot pepper sauce

1. In a small, heavy saucepan, mix the oil and flour to make a roux; cook over low heat, stirring frequently, until the roux is the color of dark mahogany, about 45 minutes. (The roux must turn very dark brown, but should not burn; do not undercook.) Reserve.

2. In a large, heavy Dutch oven, sauté the onion in 3 tablespoons of butter until soft, about 3 minutes. Stir in the okra. Cook until tender, about 3 minutes. Stir in the tomatoes; cook for 30 minutes.

3. In a large skillet, sauté the green pepper and garlic in the remaining 2 tablespoons butter for about 5 minutes. Add the shrimp. Cook until they turn pink, about 3 minutes. Add the shrimp mixture, stock, water, red pepper flakes, 2 teaspoons salt, the bay leaves, Worcestershire sauce, allspice, thyme, and reserved roux to the okra. Simmer, covered, for 1½ hours. Season to taste with salt and pepper.

4. Ladle the gumbo into soup bowls; top each serving with a scoop of rice. Pass the *filé* powder and hot pepper sauce on the side.

SERVES 8

N O T E : Filé powder is a seasoning made from dried sassafras leaves and is available in the gourmet departments of most grocery stores.

✳

SHROVE TUESDAY/PANCAKE DAY — TUESDAY BEFORE ASH WEDNESDAY

But hark, I hear the pancake bell,
And fritters make a gallant smell,
The cooks are baking, frying, boiling,
Stewing, mincing, cutting, broiling,
Carving, gormandizing, roasting,
Carbonating, cracking, slashing, toasting.

— *POOR ROBIN'S ALMANAC (1684)*

THE "PANCAKE BELL" rings out loud and clear on Shrove Tuesday, the day before Ash Wednesday, calling the religious to confession—and signaling the last day of fun and frolicking before the strict days of Lent begin. (The actual day is determined by Easter.) In England, Shrove Tuesday is also called "Pancake Day," as pancakes have long been associated with this holiday. Originally called "shriving cakes," they were eaten in conjunction with confession; the offenders were thereby "shriven" (absolved) of their iniquities. The flour in the cakes represents the staff of life; the salt, wholesomeness; the eggs, the Lenten spirit; and the milk, pure innocence.

Every year on this day, the ladies of Liberal, Kansas, hold an annual competition with the ladies of Olney, England. The competition features a footrace—with a catch. Each entrant, skillet in hand, must flip a pancake at the start of the race and then again at the finish. The fastest times are noted and compared via phone with results in Olney.

The morning of the race, there is a pancake breakfast that is open to the public, and almost 2,000 people attend. The grills used are thirty feet long and three feet wide! And according to the breakfast committee, 280 pounds of pancake mix, 35 gallons of milk, 10½ dozen eggs, and seven cups each of sugar and oil are needed to feed this amount of people! For more information, contact the Liberal Convention and Tourism Bureau at (316) 624-9425.

■ CLASSIC BREAKFAST PANCAKES ■

*I*f you are just serving three or four, and not 2,000, try this good old-fashioned buttermilk pancake recipe. If you like, sprinkle sliced fruit (or blueberries) over the surface of the cakes as soon as the batter hits the griddle.

3 eggs, separated
1 tablespoon sugar
Pinch salt
2 cups buttermilk

4 tablespoons (½ stick) unsalted butter, melted
2 cups all-purpose flour
1 teaspoon baking soda

1. In a large bowl, beat the egg yolks with the sugar and salt until light. Whisk in the buttermilk, butter, flour, and baking soda.

2. Beat the egg whites until stiff; fold into the batter.

3. Heat a lightly greased griddle or heavy skillet over medium heat. Pour about ⅓ cup batter for each cake on the griddle and cook until the underside is golden brown and the top is bubbly, about 2 minutes. Turn the pancake over and lightly brown the other side. Keep warm in a low oven while preparing the remaining pancakes.

MAKES ABOUT 12 PANCAKES

✳

ABRAHAM LINCOLN'S BIRTHDAY—
FEBRUARY 12

BORN ON FEBRUARY 12, 1809, Abraham Lincoln became the sixteenth president on March 4, 1861. He was assassinated on April 14, 1865. For a man who had such a profound effect on our country, it is truly amazing that no national celebration marks his birthday.

In New Salem, Illinois, the town where Lincoln served as storekeeper, flatboatsman, postmaster, militiaman, and legislator, there stands a reproduction of the town as Lincoln knew it. Every year his birthday is celebrated with speeches and dinners. Lincoln, it might be noted, was not a man of "gourmet" tastes. He did like his coffee, however, and there is a famous story attributed to him (and to everyone else it seems) in this regard. When once served a "dubious" cup of brew, Mr. Lincoln said to the waiter, "If this is coffee, please bring me a cup of tea, but on the other hand, if this is tea, please bring me a cup of coffee." He is also said to have liked his steak cooked well done, in the Swedish style, as served in Illinois. For more information, contact the New Salem State Park at (217) 632-4000.

■ ABRAHAM LINCOLN'S FAVORITE STEAK ■

The following recipe is adapted from Jean Anderson's Recipes from America's Restored Villages *(Doubleday & Co., 1975).*

4 shell or strip steaks, each about 1 inch
   thick
Salt and freshly ground pepper

4 teaspoons Dijon mustard
Vegetable oil
$2/3$ cup strong coffee

1. Rub the steaks with salt and pepper and then rub each side with 1 teaspoon mustard.

2. Rub a cast-iron skillet with oil and place it over medium-high heat until very hot. Sear the steaks quickly on the edges and then on both sides. Reduce the heat to low and cook for 3 to 4 minutes per side for medium-rare.

3. Remove the steaks to a platter and add the coffee to the skillet. Heat to boiling, scraping the bottom and sides of the skillet, and cook until slightly thickened. Pour over the steaks and serve.

SERVES 4

★   ★   ★

✳

HOLTVILLE CARROT FESTIVAL — SECOND WEEKEND IN FEBRUARY

HOLTVILLE, CALIFORNIA, about fifty miles west of Yuma, Arizona, calls itself the "Carrot Capital of the World." More carrots are shipped from the Holtville area than from anywhere else in the country. Come February, carrot lovers of all ages descend on the town to partake in the Holtville Carrot Festival, which has been going on for well over forty years. There is a midway with lots of rides, a tractor pull, and a livestock show. There is a cooking contest, using carrots, of course, and much of the food is available for tasting by the public. For more information, contact the Holtville Chamber of Commerce at (619) 356-2923.

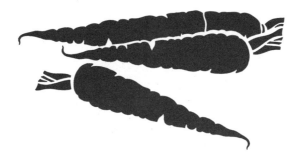

■ CARROT-NUT MARMALADE ■

*T*his is a somewhat exotic concoction that is wonderful with meats and curries. Use it like chutney. It's a great way to use up a lot of carrots.

1 pound carrots, finely shredded
Juice of 2 lemons
Finely slivered peel of 2 lemons
$\frac{1}{2}$ cup orange juice
1$\frac{1}{2}$ cups sugar

$\frac{1}{2}$ teaspoon ground cinnamon
Pinch ground cloves
$\frac{1}{4}$ cup chopped walnuts
$\frac{1}{4}$ cup sliced almonds
$\frac{1}{4}$ cup hazelnut or walnut liqueur

1. In a medium saucepan, combine the carrots, lemon juice, lemon peel, orange juice, and sugar. Let stand for 30 minutes

2. Heat the mixture to boiling; reduce the heat and cook over medium heat until the carrot becomes translucent and the syrup is quite thick, about 15 minutes. Add the cinnamon, cloves, walnuts, and almonds, and cook for 15 minutes, or until a small amount of the mixture firms up when placed on a dish that has been in the freezer.

3. Add the liqueur and mix thoroughly. Pour into hot sterilized jars. Seal. Store in a cool place or in the refrigerator.

MAKES ABOUT 2 PINTS

✳

ST. VALENTINE'S DAY— FEBRUARY 14

ST. VALENTINE'S DAY is for lovers and for those who long for love. It is a day to express your feelings for someone, openly or secretly, through notes, cards, letters, singing telegrams, and flowers—and even in the newspaper, for all to see.

It's not clear just who this St. Valentine was, since there were at least three Valentines who might have qualified for sainthood. Two—a priest and a bishop—were persecuted and murdered, and were buried together on the Flaminian Way (the Roman road between Rome and Rimini) around A.D. 269. A third Valentine, while jailed in Rome, was said to have cured his jailer's daughter of blindness. Or did he just "open her eyes" to love with love notes, as related in yet another tale? Nobody knows. There is, however, a belief, dating back to the Middle Ages, that on this day birds begin their selection process for spring mating.

In any event, Valentine's Day is a big day for florists, greeting-card retailers, and chocolatiers. (Chocolate is by far the candy of choice on this special day.)

▪ HUBERT'S WHITE CHOCOLATE MOUSSE ▪

I first tasted this dessert at Hubert's restaurant in New York. The mousse, cut into wedges and served frozen, is placed on a warm chocolate sauce that is to die for.

½ pound white chocolate
4 tablespoons (½ stick) unsalted butter
3 tablespoons light rum
3 eggs, separated

½ cup heavy cream
Hubert's Dark Chocolate Sauce (recipe
 follows)

1. Break the chocolate into pieces and place them in a large bowl with the butter and rum. Place the bowl in a very low oven (175° F or less) with the door ajar. The chocolate must melt very slowly—it should take about 45 minutes.

2. Meanwhile, in the large bowl of an electric mixer, beat the egg yolks until light and thick. Transfer the yolks to the top of a double boiler. Cook over hot water, stirring constantly, until thick. Return to the mixer bowl.

3. When the chocolate has melted, stir with a wooden spoon until smooth. Slowly beat the chocolate into the egg yolks until smooth.

4. Beat the cream until stiff. Fold into the chocolate mixture. Beat the egg whites until stiff. Fold into the mousse. Pour the mixture into a lightly oiled 8-inch springform cake pan. Cover tightly; freeze overnight.

5. Before serving, make Hubert's Dark Chocolate Sauce. Keep it warm. To serve the mousse, remove the sides from the pan. (Run a knife around the sides if necessary.) Cut the mousse into wedges. Place on cold plates. Drizzle a small amount of warm sauce over the top of each wedge, and place a puddle of sauce on either side. The wedge of mousse should look as if it is floating in a sea of dark chocolate.

SERVES 8 TO 10

HUBERT'S DARK CHOCOLATE SAUCE

½ pound semisweet chocolate
4 tablespoons (½ stick) unsalted butter
¼ cup milk, at room temperature

¼ cup heavy cream, at room
 temperature
2 tablespoons dark rum

1. Melt the chocolate in the top of a double boiler over hot water. Stir in the butter by bits.

2. Stir in the milk; add the cream and rum. Stir until smooth. Serve warm.

MAKES ABOUT 1 PINT

WASHINGTON'S BIRTHDAY/PRESIDENTS' DAY— THIRD MONDAY IN FEBRUARY

GEORGE WASHINGTON, the first president of the United States, was born on February 22, 1732, but the public observance of his birthday was moved to the third Monday of the month to create a three-day weekend. Washington's birthday is the legal holiday. Presidents' Day is, "unofficially," the combined celebration of Abraham Lincoln's and George Washington's birthdays and is observed in some states.

Every schoolchild knows the story of George Washington cutting down the cherry tree and his ensuing honesty. That the story is probably apocryphal doesn't really matter. What *does* matter is that George came from aristocracy; he was a man of cultivated manners. Although he liked to eat simply himself, he served guests lavish dinners accompanied by excellent wines, most often Madeira, the president's favorite. Martha Washington often gets credit for being a wonderful cook and keeping a book of her original recipes. She *was* a wonderful cook, but many of her recipes actually came from her first mother-in-law, Frances Parke Custis.

■ PHILADELPHIA PEPPERPOT ■

Legend has it that this soup was invented to feed George Washington and his troops while they were holed up at Valley Forge. The soup was named after the cook's hometown and became so popular that it was later sold on the streets of Philadelphia.

1 pound honeycomb tripe, washed well
1 pound veal bones or knuckles
4 cups chicken stock or broth
2 cups plus 3 tablespoons water
2 onions, finely chopped
1 clove garlic, minced
1 large stalk celery, chopped
1 large carrot, chopped
1 small green bell pepper, seeded and chopped
1 small red bell pepper, seeded and chopped
1/4 teaspoon dried thyme
1 bay leaf
1 teaspoon freshly ground pepper
6 tablespoons chopped fresh parsley
1 tablespoon cornstarch
2 potatoes, peeled and cubed
1/2 cup heavy cream (optional)
Salt and freshly ground pepper

1. Place the tripe in a large saucepan and cover with cold water. Heat to boiling; reduce the heat and simmer for 15 minutes. Drain and cool. Cut into thin strips about 1 inch long.

2. Place the veal bones in a large heavy pot or Dutch oven. Add the stock and 2 cups water. Heat to boiling, skimming the surface as needed. Add the onion, garlic, celery, carrot, bell peppers, thyme, bay leaf, ground pepper, 4 tablespoons of parsley, and the tripe. Reduce the heat and simmer, covered, for 1 hour.

3. In a small bowl, mix the cornstarch with the 3 tablespoons water until smooth. Stir into the soup. Add the potatoes and cream. Cook, uncovered, until the potatoes are tender, about 20 minutes.

4. Discard the bay leaf and remove the veal bones from the soup. If there is any meat on the bones, scrape it into the soup. Add salt and pepper to taste. Sprinkle with the remaining parsley.

SERVES 8

THE NATIONAL DATE FESTIVAL, held in the sunny desert town of Indio, California, is part of the Riverside County Fair, which draws more than a quarter of a million people during its ten-day run, beginning on Presidents' weekend. Befitting the desert fruit of Arabia, the town of Indio goes Arabian for the event. Walk into any store or bank and you are likely to find the women dressed as Arabian princesses and the men wrapped in turbans. There is much to see and do here (including ostrich and camel races), but the draw for foodies is the vast array of dates on exhibit. These include dates—with names like Amirhaji, Black Abada, Black Beauty, Honey, Medjhool, Saidy, and Thoory—that rarely find their way to the supermarket shelf. There are booths where you can sample the dates and others that demonstrate their many uses. Here, dates find their way into cereals, candies, cookies, muffins, butter, and even ice cream. For more information, contact the Riverside County National Date Festival at (619) 863-8247.

▪ DATE SHAKE ▪

There are two versions of a date shake that I am familiar with. One calls for blending ½ cup dates with 2 cups milk and ½ cup crushed ice. The richer version, and my favorite, follows.

¼ cup chopped, pitted dates   2 scoops vanilla ice cream
1 cup milk

1. Place the dates with ½ cup milk in a blender container. Blend until smooth, adding more milk if needed.

2. Add any remaining milk and the ice cream to the blender. Blend until smooth. Pour into a large glass.

SERVES 1

IN LATE FEBRUARY, more than a hundred thousand people descend on Casa Grande, Arizona (about fifty miles south of Phoenix), to celebrate O'Odham Tash, a festival that celebrates Native American Culture. The major tribes in the area are the Tohono, the O'Odham, and the Pima, but the festival is attended by tribes from as far away as Canada. Only Indians can participate in the events, but all are invited to come watch and enjoy them. Aside from the powwow, which features more than three hundred dancers of all ages, there are parades, sporting events, and a crafts fair. The featured food is Native American, and fry breads are the most popular items. At breakfast, they are served wrapped around eggs and sausage. At lunch and dinner, they are slathered with beans and topped with meat and cheese, like a tostada, or served with a red-chile stew. For dessert, you can get them sprinkled with sugar and cinnamon, or honey. For more information, contact the O'Odham Tash Festival at (602) 836-4723.

▪ RED-CHILE STEW ▪

If you can't find ground chiles in your neck of the woods, you can use chili powder, but beware: Most commercial chili powders already contain some oregano and cumin, so adjust the recipes accordingly. I serve this on rice.

2 tablespoons vegetable oil, lard, or
  bacon drippings
1½ pounds boneless chuck, finely
  chopped
1 tablespoon all-purpose flour
2 cups chicken broth or water

¼ cup ground red chiles (mild or hot)
1 large fresh clove garlic, minced
Pinch dried oregano
½ teaspoon ground cumin
Salt to taste

1. Heat the oil in a medium pot over high heat until hot. Add the chuck and sauté, stirring constantly, until the meat loses its pink color, 4 or 5 minutes.

2. Sprinkle the meat with the flour and cook, stirring constantly, over medium-low heat for 2 minutes. Stir in 1 cup of broth, scraping the bottom and sides of the pan, until smooth. Add the ground chiles, garlic, oregano, and cumin. Stir until smooth and add the remaining 1 cup broth. Heat to boiling; reduce the heat. Cook, covered, until the beef is tender and the stew is thick, about 1 hour and 15 minutes. Add salt to taste.

SERVES 2 TO 4

★ ★ ★

■ LEAP YEAR DAY—FEBRUARY 29 ■

Once every four years, an extra day is added to the calendar to bring it in line with the earth's orbital clock, which is approximately 365.2422 days. This means that each year, five hours and forty-eight minutes extra just hang in limbo until Leap Year comes along. Leap years occur every four years, except in century years that are not divisible by 400.

✳

★ ★ ★

SELECT BIBLIOGRAPHY

✳

The American Book of Days. George William Douglas, A.M., Litt.D. The H. W. Wilson Company, New York, 1937.

The American Heritage Cookbook. The editors of American Heritage. American Heritage Publishing, New York, 1964.

California Festivals, second edition. Carl and Katie Landau with Kathy Kincade. Landau Communications, San Francisco, 1990.

Celebrations. Robert J. Myers with the editors of Hallmark Cards. Doubleday & Company, Garden City, New York, 1972.

Chase's Annual Events: The Day-By-Day Directory to 1992. Edited and compiled by Contemporary Books, Chicago, 1991.

Colonial Virginia Cookery. Jane Carson. The Colonial Williamsburg Foundation, Williamsburg, Virginia, 1985.

Curious Customs. Tad Tuleja. Harmony Books, New York, 1987.

The Dictionary of American Food and Drink. John F. Mariani. Ticknor & Fields, New Haven and New York, 1983.

Eating in America. Waverley Root and Richard de Rochemont. William Morrow & Co., New York, 1976.

A Feast of Festivals. Joanne Taylor Hane, C.F.E., and Catherine L. Holshouser for The International Festivals Association. CelestialArts, Berkeley, 1990.

Festivals of New England. Kathy Kincade and Carl Landau. Landau Communications, San Francisco, 1989.

Festivals of the Pacific Northwest. Kathy Kincade and Steve Rank. Landau Communications, San Francisco, 1990.

Festivals of the Southwest. Kathy Kincade and Carl Landau. Landau Communications, San Francisco, 1990.

Festivals U.S.A. Kathleen Thompson Hill. John Wiley & Sons, Inc., New York, 1988.

The Folklore of American Holidays, second edition. Edited by Hennig Cohen and Tristram Potter Coffin. Gale Research Inc., Detroit, 1991.

Food Festival. Alice M. Geffen and Carole Berglie. Pantheon Books, New York, 1986.

The Food Professional's Guide. Compiled by Irena Chalmers for the James Beard Foundation. American Showcase, Inc., New York, 1990.

Foods from Harvest Festivals and Folk Fairs. Anita Borghese. Thomas Y. Crowell Company, New York, 1977.

The Hero in America. Dixon Wecter. Ann Arbor Paperbacks, University of Michigan Press, 1966.

Holidays. Edited by Trevor Nevitt Dupuy. Franklin Watts, Inc., New York, 1965.

Holidays and Anniversaries of the World, second edition. Edited by Jennifer Mossman. Gale Research Inc., Detroit, 1990.

The Illuminated Book of Days. Edited by Kay and Marshall Lee, with illustrations by Kate Greenaway and Eugene Grasset. G. P. Putnam's Sons, New York, 1979.

The Jewish Festival Cookbook. Fannie Engle and Gertrude Blair. David McKay Company, Inc., New York, 1954.

The Jewish Holiday Kitchen (new and expanded edition). Joan Nathan. Schocken Books, New York, 1988.

Kwanzaa (revised edition). Cedric McClester. Gumbs & Thomas, New York, 1990.

Legends, Lies & Cherished Myths of American History. Richard Shenkman. Harper & Row, Publishers, New York, 1989.

A Treasury of American Folklore. Edited by B. A. Botkin. Crown Publishers, New York, 1944.

INDEX

✺

ABOUT THE AUTHOR

Phillip Stephen Schulz received his culinary training while working with the late Bert Greene at The Store in Amagansett, Long Island. After The Store's closing, in 1976, he worked with Greene developing and testing recipes for five Bert Greene cookbooks. He is a member of the International Association of Culinary Professionals (IACP).

Schulz has written for many publications and is the author of six cookbooks, including *America the Beautiful Cookbook,* winner of both the IACP and James Beard awards, *As American as Apple Pie, Cooking with Fire & Smoke, Cooking for Giving* (with Bert Greene), and *Vodka 'n' Vittles.*

He lives in New York City.